MA
DEI
RA

T0043361

Travel with Marco Polo
Insider Tips

INSIDER TIP
Your shortcut
to a great
experience

MARCO POLO
TOP HIGHLIGHTS

MERCADO DOS LAVRADORES ⭐

The market halls in the heart of Funchal, with their exotic fruits, vegetables, fish, wickerwork and flowers, are a treat for the eye, nose and palate.

📷 *Tip: On Fridays the farmers fill the inner courtyard with their produce.*

➤ p. 46, Funchal

JARDIM TROPICAL MONTE PALACE ⭐

Kitsch fairy-tale park or artistic tropical garden? Whatever your verdict, the palace garden of Monte is simply amazing.

📷 *Tip: Wait for the swans to pose in front of the sculptures and the former Palace Hotel.*

➤ p. 50, Funchal

CABLE CAR ⭐

Take a trip over the roofs of Funchal up to Monte.

➤ p. 47, Funchal

FANAL ⭐

Ancient laurel trees, lush forests, spectacular views and beautiful hiking trails surround the Fanal forestry station.

📷 *Tip: In the fog, the centuries-old laurel trees turn into an enchanted fairy wood.*

➤ p. 78, The North

PAÚL DA SERRA ⭐

Discover a high moorland landscape in a harsh climate similar to the Scottish Highlands. There are breathtaking views into the valleys from the plateau at above 1,000m.

➤ p. 68, The Southwest

LAVA POOLS ⭐

Porto Moniz on the northwest coast has the most beautiful natural pools on Madeira, created from volcanic rock.

📷 *Tip: When the waves crash onto the rocks and the spray is blown into the pools, it makes for a spectacular photograph.*

➤ p. 77, The North

PONTA DE SÃO LOURENÇO ⭐

A hiking trails leads across this fascinating promontory in the east.

📷 *Tip: The rocky scenery, which can be all shades from red to yellow, is best snapped from the Miradouro Ponta do Rosto.*

➤ p. 100, The East

PRAIA DO PORTO SANTO ⭐

Porto Santo's south coast has what most of Madeira is lacking: a golden sandy beach that stretches as far as the eye can see.

➤ p. 108, Porto Santo

PICO RUIVO, PICO DO ARIEIRO ⭐

A hike to two of Madeira's highest peaks will be rewarded with fabulous views of the volcanic landscape (photo).

📷 *Tip: Take great pictures of the "Stairway to Heaven" by the rocks behind the Pedra Rija.*

➤ p. 84, The North,
➤ p. 115, Discovery Tours

FESTA DA FLOR 🔟

Every spring, Funchal hosts a creative and colourful flower festival.

📷 *Tip: Avoid the crowds and seek out the decorated floats and dressed-up children in the set-up area ahead of the procession.*

➤ p. 131, Festivals & Events

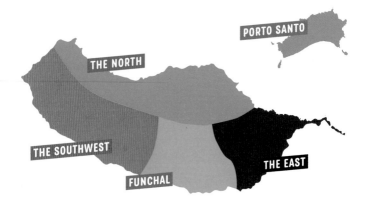

⟳	Plan your visit	⫴	Eating/drinking	🌂	Rainy day activities
€-€€€	Price categories	👜	Shopping	🐷	Budget activities
(*)	Premium-rate phone number	⏃	Going out	👪	Family activities
		🏖	Top beaches	⚑	Classic experiences

(📖 A2) Refers to the removable pull-out map
(0) Located off the map
The pull-out map includes a plan of the bus routes on Madeira.

BEST OF
MADEIRA

Terraced fields near Boaventura

BEST ☂

WHEN IT RAINS

RETRACING THE STEPS OF CR7
Fans of Funchal's most famous son, football superstar Cristiano Ronaldo, will be overjoyed with *Museu CR7*, where his life story and road to success are presented in a vivid and interactive manner.
➤ p. 43, Funchal

UNWIND WITH A CUP OF TEA
When rain from the Atlantic blankets the island, the *Loja do Chá* in Funchal is the perfect retreat. This inviting tea house also offers apple pie and scones. Their cosy wicker chairs are ideal to while away an afternoon.
➤ p. 52, Funchal

SHOP LIKE A LOCAL
Madeira Shopping seems to be where the whole island comes to shop. Mix with the locals in the cinemas, cafés, restaurants and more than 100 shops at the island's largest shopping mall.
➤ p. 53, Funchal

ART & CULTURE IN CALHETA
Mudas. Museu de Arte Contempôranea has attracted much attention for its bold architecture. It is also home to exhibitions, an innovative cultural programme and an excellent café-restaurant.
➤ p. 66, The Southwest

SEE THE FISH FROM DRY LAND
What used to be a fort in Porto Moniz is now home to the *Aquário da Madeira*, where almost all of Madeira's marine life cavorts before your eyes (photo).
➤ p. 76, The North

AMAZING WHALES
You can easily spend half a rainy day in the excellent *Museu da Baleia* in Caniçal, where exciting films tell the story of the whales, including why and how sperm whales were hunted off Madeira in centuries past.
➤ p. 99, The East

BEST

ON A BUDGET

FOR SMALLER WALLETS

SWEET TREATS FROM THE CANE

At one time, sugar cane made the island's plantation owners rich. Today, there are only a few sugar-cane mills still in use on Madeira. One of them is run by the *Sociedade dos Engenhos da Calheta*. In this mill, you can see how they make rum and syrup – and taste them both for a small fee.

➤ p. 65, The Southwest

A BEACON OF LIGHT AT NIGHT

Madeira's most attractive lighthouse stands at the tip of the Rocha da Vigia in *Ponta do Pargo*. Constructed in 1922, it lures visitors inside to see its photo *exhibition* depicting the island's other beacons of light.

➤ p. 70, The Southwest

HOMES FROM THE PAST

The village of *Santana* preserves the traditional *casas de colmo*, distinctive wooden dwellings with red doors, blue-framed windows, green shutters and steeply sloping thatched roofs. The historic houses make the past come alive – like a trip to a museum, but for free.

➤ p. 83, The North

A GARDEN TO DIE FOR

The *Quinta Splendida* hotel in Caniço has a wonderful garden in which many plants are helpfully labelled. Hotel guests as well as the general public can enjoy its beauty and the fabulous ocean views (photo).

➤ p. 93, The East

FREE ENTRY

Admission to the museums of Funchal is free on 18 May (World Museum Day) and 27 September (World Tourism Day). Apart from that, many museums are free to visit on Sundays.

➤ p. 134, Good to know

BEST

WITH CHILDREN

FUN FOR YOUNG & OLD

PLAYFUL EXPLORATION

The *Madeira Story Centre* is a fascinating museum; its exhibits on Madeira's geology, discovery and settlement are laid out in a playful interactive format.
➤ p. 48, Funchal

BLAST FROM THE PAST

The *Museu do Brinquedo* displays children's toys from the past and will surely make many adults feel nostalgic for their own childhoods.
➤ p. 48, Funchal

SETTING SAIL

Children's eyes light up at the sight of the *Santa Maria de Colombo*, a replica of Christopher Columbus's ship. Once aboard, you will quickly feel like an explorer yourself – and possibly spot a few dolphins!
➤ p. 53, Funchal

INSIDE THE VOLCANO

In *Grutas de São Vicente* you are guided through a fascinating system of lava tunnels which are 890,000 years old. Take a lift from the visitor centre down to the centre of the earth. How will you get back to the surface? Find out in the 3D cinema!
➤ p. 81, The North

A GHOST TRAIN TO THE PAST

In the *Parque Temático da Madeira* in Santana, children can enjoy trampolines, pedal boats and a ride on a ghost train – together with the seafarers who discovered the island.
➤ p. 83, The North

WATER & WINGS

Water slides, man-made streams and bathing pools – the *Aquaparque* of Santa Cruz is great (and wet) fun for the entire family. You can also admire reptiles, parrots and birds of prey.
➤ p. 96, The East

BEST ⚑

CLASSIC EXPERIENCES

ONLY ON MADEIRA

THE OLDER, THE BETTER

This applies to the island's most precious drink: Madeira wine! A visit to *Blandy's Wine Lodge* in Funchal will allow you to learn how this liquid gold is produced, and you can taste it as well.
➤ p. 31, Shopping

ISLAND OF ETERNAL SPRING

In Funchal's *Jardim Botânico* you will quickly discover why Madeira is called the island of eternal spring. More than 2,500 tropical and subtropical plants show off their colours in this botanical garden (photo).
➤ p. 48, Funchal

SLEDGE WITHOUT SNOW

Take one of the famous *basket sledges* on runners, propelled by strong local men, along the road from Monte down towards Funchal.
➤ p. 49, Funchal

ESPADA & ESPETADA

Madeira's national dishes are true delicacies: try the famous black scabbard fish *(espada)* in Santana's *Serra e Mar*. The traditional *espetada* – juicy beef on a skewer – can be enjoyed at *A Carreta* in Ponta do Pargo.
➤ p. 71, The Southwest, p. 84, The North

POOLS OF VOLCANIC ROCK

The surf crashes on the rocks a few metres away while you take a relaxed swim in the natural *lava pools* of Porto Moniz – an extraordinary experience!
➤ p. 77, The North

ALONG THE LEVADAS

Walk alongside ancient irrigation channels through woods of eucalyptus and laurel, past dizzying gorges or along broad forest tracks. The paths on the *levadas* of Madeira, for example on the *Levada do Furado*, are unforgettable.
➤ p. 94, The East

GET TO KNOW MADEIRA

Basket-sledge ride in Monte, Funchal

DISCOVER MADEIRA

Agapanthus (African lily) framing the view of Machico

Island of Flowers, Pearl of the Atlantic, Island of Eternal Spring – Madeira has so many names! One thing is certain: a single holiday is definitely not enough to discover its astonishing variety of landscapes and hiking trails, as well as the incredible mix of culture, activities, excellent cuisine and natural wonders. And don't forget the countless flowers …

MOUNTAINS & SO MUCH MORE

Madeira has much more to offer than flower beds – although there is nothing wrong with the beautiful parks and gardens! The island is a paradise for anyone who loves marine and mountain landscapes and enjoys strolling through charming villages and mingling in the crowd at lively festivals. And outdoor enthusisasts are in for a treat too, with great hiking, golf, hang-gliding, surfing,

1419/20
Portuguese navigators discover Porto Santo and Madeira

From 1423
Initial settlements, many years of slash-and-burn and the beginning of sugar cane and wine production

1703
The Methuen Treaty transfers the wine business to British ownership

1860/61 and 1893/94
Empress Elisabeth of Austria ('Sisi') lives on Madeira for a few months, starting a fashionable trend for European elites

1960/64
Airports are opened on Porto Santo and Madeira

scuba diving, mountaineering, canyoning and mountain biking available. And you can cool down after any strenuous activity by jumping into the cool waters of the Atlantic Ocean from pebble or black sandy beaches, or into the natural lava pools. There are even golden sandy beaches – imported from Morocco! A "real" sandy beach several kilometres long can be found on the sister island of Porto Santo. That Madeira does not offer Balearic-style beaches is no shortcoming, but more an advantage. The majority of holidaymakers are here for the natural beauty of the island, the friendliness of its inhabitants and the good food, and not so much for the sangria. But anyone who thinks that nothing ever happens in Funchal should walk through the old town in the evening – the Madeirans certainly know how to celebrate in style.

WHAT ABOUT THE ETERNAL SPRING?

Unfortunately, things are not quite that simple. Nowadays, the summers are pretty hot and dry (thanks to climate change), and forest fires are sadly on the increase. In the winter, it is generally pleasantly mild and, with a bit of luck, you can catch a period of sunny days with temperatures ranging between 15 and 20°C. But at some point it has to rain. Rainy periods can occur at any time in autumn, winter and spring, but take them in your stride. First of all, the Pearl of the Atlantic needs the rain, otherwise it would not be so green, you would not find all the colourful fruit in the market hall and the gardens would only feature cacti … What is more,

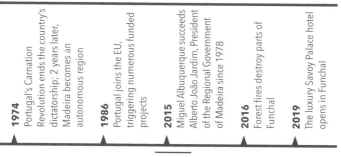

1974
Portugal's Carnation Revolution ends the country's dictatorship; 2 years later, Madeira becomes an autonomous region

1986
Portugal joins the EU, triggering numerous funded projects

2015
Miguel Albuquerque succeeds Alberto João Jardim, President of the Regional Government of Madeira since 1978

2016
Forest fires destroy parts of Funchal

2019
The luxury Savoy Palace hotel opens in Funchal

if it is raining and windy on one side of the island, the weather can still be good on the other side! The damp Passat clouds prefer to congregate around the north face of the island's mountains while there are perfect weather conditions on the southern side or in lower-lying areas. This explains the verdant scenery, particularly in the north. The laurel forest of Madeira is such an outstanding feature that it was declared a World Heritage Site by UNESCO in 1999. This unique so-called *laurisilva* still covers around 20 per cent of the island and is a relic of the laurel forest vegetation that was also found in Central Europe before the Ice Ages.

HIKE ALONGSIDE WATER COURSES

The first settlers arrived on the island in the 15th century and were quick to recognise the influence of altitude and orientation on agriculture and irrigation in different parts of the island. They began channelling water from the higher regions in the north to the sugar-cane plantations and terraced fields in the sunny southern regions, which were often too dry. This was the birth of the levada system. The settlers lost no time in creating daring water courses through the rocks to direct valuable rain and spring water from A to B. Thanks to its *levadas*, today Madeira is an ideal island for hiking. The *levada* maintenance tracks created an extensive network of paths leading both the *levada* workers and enthusiastic tourists into the depths of the island's green heart with its wild gorges and rock formations that are millions of years old. Every twist and turn reveals a new breathtaking panorama, especially in the fantastic laurel forest.

OPPOSITES ATTRACT

An excellent road network ensures that every corner of the island can be reached quickly. Madeira is an archipelago full of contrasts and surprises: Porto Santo has dry mountain slopes and an endless golden sandy beach, while the Ilhas Desertas feature uninhabited rocky plains. Visitors are confronted by a massively developed southern region (largely covered in concrete) thanks to generous EU funding), but there are also huge national parks in the interior of the island and a largely unspoilt northern region. For many years now, Funchal has been considered the cleanest city in Portugal, and all villages and towns are constantly smartening themselves up; there are no better-maintained front gardens and municipal parks in the entire country. You will experience heavy rainfall, but the sun will be shining in a clear blue sky only a short time later. You can hike through a dry headland one day, through a luscious laurel forest the next day and wander through decadently blooming gardens the day after that. Allow yourself to be enchanted by the beauty of nature on the archipelago, by its cordial inhabitants and their delicious recipes. And don't forget: if the weather doesn't live up to your expectations, simply hop over to the other side of the island: you are bound to find your "permanent spring" somewhere!

INSIDER TIP
It's always spring somewhere on Madeira

AT A GLANCE

251,000
inhabitants (2021)

Southampton: 249,000 (2021)

850km
distance to the Portuguese mainland

150km
coastline (only Madeira)

Isle of Wight: 92km

800km²
area

London: 1,572km²

HIGHEST PEAK: PICO RUIVO

1,862m

MAXIMUM TEMPERATURE

AUGUST 26°C

WATER TEMPERATURE OF THE ATLANTIC IN JANUARY

18°C

English Channel: 10°C

RANGE OF THE LIGHTHOUSE OF PONTA DO PARGO:
28 nautical miles (52km)
Needles Lighthouse (Isle of Wight): 17 nautical miles (31km)

LEVADA

The *levada* network covers 2,500km

RONALDO'S "GOLDEN BALLS":
2008, 2013, 2014, 2016, 2017

ALCOHOL CONTENT IN MADEIRA WINE:
17–22 %

UNDERSTAND MADEIRA

Festival in May, with its grand procession of brightly decorated floats and girls with flowers in Funchal and the luscious carpets of flowers under the lilac blooms of the jacaranda trees.

FLOWERY DREAMS

No advertising text for the "Island of Flowers" fails to mention the "swimming garden in the Atlantic". This raises the expectations of some visitors who get off the plane and expect to see a carpet of flowers as far as the eye can see, ideally any time between January and December … That is unrealistic, particularly on the heavily built-up south coast, so please don't be disappointed. However, thanks to irrigation, many plants frequently found in subtropical and temperate climates grow on Madeira in the lovingly cultivated front gardens and parks. Not everything flowers at the same time, but you are always sure to see something in bloom, even in winter! Around 800 different native plants and over 500 imported plant species are found on the island, and since the 1980s, two-thirds of its area has been designated as a nature reserve.

In the terraced fields you can discover grape vines, bananas, potatoes and beans alongside a wealth of exotic fruits. Nearly all year long, aloe plants, hydrangeas and lilies of all types and colours line the winding roads, and the aroma of wild herbs is omnipresent in the mountains in early summer. The absolute highlight for flower lovers is the annual *Flower*

MAINLAND PORTUGUESE

Some things aren't so easy on an island. Occasionally, the Madeirans feel somewhat remote and isolated, even today, almost 50 years after Salazar's dictatorship. During that period, between the 1930s and the Carnation Revolution of 1974, Madeira was left very much to its own political and economic devices. However, even in the 21st century there are certain limitations: shopping in a well-known Swedish furniture store? Only possible on the mainland. Going to rock concerts? Only in Lisbon, which is 1,000km away. Despite low-cost flights and discounted tickets for island inhabitants and VAT at 22% instead of 23%, a latent feeling of discrimination remains. Perhaps this is partly because the mainland Portuguese make fun of the islanders' dialect or because the central government in Lisbon controls all decisions made by the parliament on Madeira, despite the fact that the archipelago was granted the special status of an autonomous region in 1976 and has its own elected president.

It will be interesting to see what the future brings, and whether the Portuguese of the mainland and the islands become closer to each other – prompted perhaps by the tourism sector.

FESTIVAL LOVERS

You will hardly find a weekend without some sort of procession or harvest festival for a specific kind of fruit or vegetable! The Madeirans will always find a reason to celebrate, whether it is the chestnut festival, a wine festival or a celebration of bananas, cherries or lemons. On top of that, there are frequent festivals for patron saints and local chapels! Since not that much else is happening on the island, a street or village festival provides a change from daily life. These celebrations are accompanied with stalls selling succulent meat skewers and performances by folklore groups. If you happen to visit the onion festival, don't miss the fantastic onion exhibition set up by farmers!

GLAZED WALLS

There is hardly a single church without ⚑ *azulejos*: Portugal's ceramic tiles are also a part of Madeira's building tradition. The oldest examples originate from the 17th century, but even today walls are decorated with the weatherproof tiles that are much more than mere decoration. Introduced by the Moors, *al-zulij* translates as "little stone". *Azulejos*, frequently patterned in blue and white but also sometimes colourfully decorated, are excellent for protecting walls from damage through heat and harsh weather conditions.

MADEIRA BRITS

Madeira almost ended up as a British island, but the English instead chose Tangier and Bombay as a dowry when

Parish festival in Ribeira Brava

King Charles II married Princess Catarina of Bragança in 1660. Still, the British are omnipresent on Madeira (and not only as tourists): they have exerted a great influence on wine growing and still control almost the entire Madeira wine production. And who was it who made white embroidery and basket-making internationally popular? Involved also in the biggest daily newspaper, numerous travel agencies and hotels, the British currently appear to own half of the island.

MANUEL'S ORNAMENTATION

If you have already visited Portugal, you will surely have heard of King Manuel I – also known as the "Fortunate", as the Portuguese experienced the zenith of their world renown and wealth during his reign (1495–1521). This was thanks to the successful voyages of discovery and conquest undertaken by Vasco da Gama and other seafarers. Madeira had been discovered a few decades previously, and during this period an intense building boom commenced on the island. Based on the treasures he amassed through his maritime power, Manuel was able to finance the construction of magnificent monasteries, churches, towers and palaces ornamented with delicate maritime decoration across the whole of Portugal.

You can still see churches and chapels decorated with typical symbols of the Manueline period: gateways are ornamented with  stone decorations in the form of ships' ropes, algae and corals; balustrades are decorated with the Crusaders' Maltese cross; and Manuel's own favourite symbol crops up time and time again: the armillary sphere, the navigational instrument which became well known under Prince Henry the Navigator.

WATER CHANNELS

Some channels lead through the middle of settlements (even through Funchal) and flow alongside sloping vineyards and cultivated terraces, while others run through deep valleys and dense laurel forests or through narrow tunnels. You can take a relaxed

Madeira's *levadas*, like this one in Rabacal, carry a steady flow of irrigation water

walk alongside some of these water channels, but with others you have to be really careful not to lose your balance at narrow points where the path suddenly disappears – sometimes there is also a steep drop. These are the fantastic *levadas*, the pride of Madeira! Shortly after the island was discovered, slaves were charged with the task of creating these man-made irrigation channels to lead water from remote springs down to the sugarcane plantations. Part of this network, which has a total length of around 2,500km, is connected to hydropower plants and used to generate electricity.

WRECKS

Warm, clean, turquoise water, as well as a marine reserve around the offshore rocky islands; there's no doubt that Porto Santo is ideal for scuba diving. It also has three ships that you can explore under the water! The *Madeirense*, a passenger ship built in 1961, was deliberately sunk in 2000. Corals and fish have since settled in this artificial reef at a depth of 30m. In 2016, after several decades of service in the Portuguese Navy, the corvette *General Pereira D`Eça* joined the first wreck. Such wrecking operations require meticulous planning because the team responsible needs to make sure that the ships are in exactly the right position so that divers can safely explore the wrecks and that no toxic substances can damage the marine environment. Feedback has been so positive that Madeira has now sunk another former navy vessel: the

TRUE OR FALSE?

RONALDO ISLAND

You have landed at the Aeroporto Cristiano Ronaldo, have no doubt taken selfies with the funny bust in front of the terminal and the virile statue in front of his CR7 Museum, or perhaps you are staying at the CR7 Hotel? What next? Is the island going to be renamed after him … Talking with local people, the topic inevitably turns to him. How do Madeirans cope with this? Well, as the island is the home of this man who was named World Player of the Year several times, every goal of his is worshipped here. Nothing is going to diminish their Golden Boy!

FLOWER LOVERS

Madeira – the legendary "Island of Flowers" where the land is covered in blooms as far as the eye can see … Hang on: the south coast is more or less covered in concrete, and then there are all the roads, towns and residential properties! Where are all those flowers? They can be found in both the public and private parks and along the *avenidas* and scenic routes. And, of course, in all the beautiful front gardens, because the islanders are genuine flower lovers who take great care of their beloved plants. Even if they don't have a garden themselves, you will see lots of pots in the street by the front doors.

Corveta Afonso Cerqueira , which was in use until recently, is now on the seabed off Cabo Girão and countless fish have quickly taken to it.

INSIDER TIP
Explore the wrecks

BEAUTIFUL LIVING

You will see *quintas* on many hillside locations in Madeira: grand mansions and properties which were mainly constructed during the 18th and 19th centuries. This was the golden age of the wine trade, when numerous British merchants settled on Madeira; they were presumably impervious to the frequently damp and clammy climate in Monte, Santo da Serra or other smart locations. They employed international architects to design their fashionable properties and create exotic vegetation around them. Some of these magnificent parks can still be visited today, and many of the *quintas* have now been converted into hotels. This exquisite architectural heritage stands in stark contrast to the island's extensive building mania – chiefly funded by money from the EU – and perhaps you would genuinely prefer to stay in a restored *quinta* with a romantic garden than in a concrete box on the coast!

OVER THE HILLS

Imagine that you have been slaving away for years to make a profit from your vineyards – and then your grapes are destroyed by phylloxera or mildew. You would then perhaps leave the area and make a new start somewhere else. This is what happened to numerous inhabitants of 19th-century Madeira who lost their vineyards through blight, and resettled in Brazil, Venezuela, South Africa, England and the Channel Islands. Madeira has been familiar with the phenomenon of emigration and return migration since the earliest settlements on the island (actually the "emigration" of the Portuguese from the poorer parts of mainland Portugal) – natural catastrophes, economic crises or changed working conditions have repeatedly caused the island inhabitants to seek their fortune elsewhere.

The current total population of the archipelago is around 260,000, but there are around a million "Madeirans" who originate directly or indirectly from the island. Some emigrants return after a period of time, frequently establishing a small business with the money earned abroad. If you see a magnificent new house next to a modest parental home in the villages, this is mostly a clear sign of emigrants who have returned.

RAISE YOUR GLASSES

An easy question for a quiz: name a typical drink from Madeira. The first answer is sure to be the tasty Madeira wine which has also found its way into our cuisine in various forms. This liqueur wine with around 20% alcohol is made by adding brandy to stop the fermentation of the wine must, meaning that a large proportion of fructose is retained. The remainder of the secret is the storage in warm attics (the so-called *Cantiero* process) or the heating of grape juice in steel tanks

(*Estufagem* method). You will recognise which of these processes has been used to make your Madeira wine by the price and taste: you will pay at least 30 euros for wine from one of the noble grape types – Sercial (dry), Verdelho (medium dry), Boal (medium sweet) and Malvasia (sweet) – seasoned for 15 years in oak casks in warm attics; whereas a bottle of Madeira made from the common grape Tinta Negra Mole seasoned in steel tanks will only cost 3 euros.

WINGS & FINS

The extent of Madeira's fauna is fairly modest, as few types of animals succeeded in reaching the archipelago independently; in fact, only bats, insects and birds managed to make their own way to the island. These were also joined by a few common wall lizards who multiplied in huge numbers, as you can observe today on sunny walls throughout the island. In picnic areas, you will also frequently be accompanied by the Madeira chaffinch waiting for some crumbs; it's one of around 200 bird species found on Madeira.

Marine fauna displays much greater variety – ranging from black scabbard fish to tuna and cephalopods. Occasionally, whales and dolphins can be observed, and even the previously endangered monk seals have returned to the island. You will rarely catch sight of most of the livestock – which were all imported to the island: pigs live in their pigsties and cows and goats are normally kept in traditional huts with pointed roofs.

The extensive laurel forests are the habitat of the Madeira chaffinch

EATING
SHOPPING
SPORT

Funchal, Mercado dos Lavradores

EATING & DRINKING

Rustic and plentiful – Madeiran cooking still revolves around down-to-earth fish and meat dishes; anything else is more or less regarded as a snack by Madeirans!

A GOOD START

You have hardly sat down at the table when the waiter arrives with a basket of *bolo do caco*, a warm and lovely smelling wheat bread with garlic butter. On Madeira, the so-called *couvert* (cover) usually comprises a version of the traditional bread; it can also include olives, cheese, ham or prawns. Strictly speaking, the waiter should ask you whether you actually want all of this (because if you keep it, you also have to pay for it), but some waiters happily serve it to you without question. If you do not want these starters, just hand them back with a smile.

GOOD OR A LOT OR BOTH?

In the island's traditional peasant cooking, "good" is synonymous with "plentiful". With a little luck you will find tasty, down-to-earth specialities such as wheat soup or watercress soup *(sopa de trigo, sopa de agriões)*, boiled kid *(cabrito)* and pork with wine and garlic *(carne vinho e alhos)* in a village restaurant or *tasca* (pub). The cooks in tourist hotels and restaurants stick to standard international fare, while French, Far Eastern and fusion cuisine are the main styles in gourmet restaurants, where food is colourful and artistically presented but you may not feel that there is enough on your plate.

FISH & MEAT

The twin pillars of the island's food are *espada* and *espetada* – scabbard fish and skewered beef. Another popular main course is tuna *(atum)*, often served in a strong onion sauce.

Espetada, sonhos, avocado (left), a plate of *lapas* (right)

Swordfish *(espadarte)*, grouper *(garoupa)* and various types of bream also feature on the menu. Almost all restaurants serve limpets *(lapas)*. Fresh mountain trout *(truta)* makes a delicious change from seafish. They are farmed in Ribeiro Frio.

WHAT MADEIRANS LIKE

Madeirans prefer *frango* and *bife* – chicken and beef – to fish, which is fairly expensive. At celebrations, it is usual for dozens of whole chickens to be sizzling on the grill as an alternative to *espetada*. Unfortunately, almost all the chickens are intensively farmed. Madeirans often eat their beef in the form of sandwiches. A large proportion of beef is imported – and the same is true of pork.

Vegetarians (and vegans) are still a bit of an alien species in Portugal, but modern chefs have recognised the signs of changing times and are offering a range of meat-free dishes. Funchal has a few wholly vegetarian restaurants (see the list at: *happycow. net*).

A POTPOURRI OF SIDE DISHES

The main supplement to meat are potatoes, boiled or as French fries. Often on the menu are sweet potatoes baked in their skins *(batata doce)* or *milho frito* (polenta, seasoned with herbs and diced). *Inhame*, a member of the yam family, is also available. When it comes to vegetables, carrots and beans from the island's gardens are much in evidence; sometimes a restaurant owner dishes up *pimpinela* (chayote, a kind of pale green gourd), which is often eaten at home.

E PARA BEBER? (WHAT WOULD YOU LIKE TO DRINK?)

Madeira produces really good beer, with the leading brand being "Coral", which is also popular on the Portuguese mainland. If you want beer on draught, ask for an *imperial*. It is often mixed with lemonade to make shandy. The island's table wine, which enthusiastic winemakers have been

A typical non-alcoholic drink is "Brisa": this fruity sparkling drink comes in various flavours, passion fruit being by far the tastiest.

A sweet delicacy: *bolo de mel*

producing for about ten years now, is still drunk relatively little, and wines brought in from Portugal are more common.

At festivals, local wines – light-heartedly known on Madeira as *café de setembro*, September coffee – come into their own. Their taste is somewhere between earthy and sour, which is why the Madeirans tend to mix them with lemonade. In Santo da Serra and Camacha there is another traditional mixed drink: *cidra*, i.e. cider, to which sugar or honey is added. *Poncha* is a popular pre-dinner drink, and some people order a glass of sweet Madeira wine for dessert.

SWEET SEDUCTION

Quer sobremesa? There's no escaping the question about dessert, and on Madeira the answer is generally yes. Home-made cakes *(bolos)*, passion-fruit pudding, crème caramel or fresh fruit are the usual choices.

AFTERWARDS, COFFEE & TEA

After a meal, Madeirans always order coffee. If they like it small and black, they order a *bica* (espresso) or a *bica curta* (the even stronger version). If they prefer to dilute their coffee with a little milk, they ask for a *garoto*. A larger milky coffee is known as a *chinesa*. The *galão*, which is served in a glass, resembles a latte macchiato.

A brew made from lemon rind and hot water is called *chá de limão* on the island. This drink, and coffee too, are available as *pingado* – with a shot of spirits, usually whisky.

A CONTA, SE FAZ FAVOR!

When it's time to pay the bill, "one for all" is the guiding principle. It is not normal for each guest to pay separately: either the guests divide the amount among themselves, or those who don't pay will take their turn next time the group eats out. If you do wish to pay separately, you should ask the waiter for *"A conta em separado, se faz favor"*.

TODAY'S SPECIALS

Starters

BOLO DO CACO
Warm bread made from wheat flour
with garlic butter

SOPA DE TOMATE
Creamy tomato soup with a
poached egg

LAPAS GRELHADAS
Grilled limpets with garlic butter
and lemon juice

CASTANHETAS
Small fish similar to anchovies,
fried and tossed in garlic oil

Main courses

PEIXE ESPADA COM BANANA
Black scabbard fish, filleted and
breaded, with banana

ESPETADA REGIONAL
Beef, rolled in coarse-grained bay-leaf
salt and grilled on a skewer

ARROZ DE MARISCO
A stew made from rice, fish and
other seafood

BIFE DE ATUM COM MILHO FRITO
Tuna steak with fried polenta

CARNE DE VINHO E ALHOS
Diced pork, marinated in wine and
vinegar with garlic

Desserts & cake

PUDIM DE MARACUJÁ
Creamy passion fruit pudding made
from locally grown fruit

BOLO DE MEL
A dark, spiced cake containing
sugar-cane syrup

TARTE DE MAÇÃ
Apple tart

Drinks

VINHO DA MADEIRA
Madeira wine, dry as an aperitif or
sweet as a dessert wine

CERVEJA CORAL
Local beer brewed near
Câmara de Lobos

PONCHA
Mini-cocktail made from sugar-cane
spirit, honey and freshly pressed
orange and lemon juice

CAFÉ/BICA
A small cup of strong coffee

SHOPPING

DELICIOUS SOUVENIRS

The best souvenirs are always edible. Apart from Madeira wine (see below), why not get a jar of flower honey plus a small bottle of sugar-cane spirit in order to mix yourself a delicious *poncha* at home. (We always think the ready-made ponchas have a rather artificial taste). You can always serve the spicy *bolo de mel* (gingerbread made from sugar-cane syrup) next Christmas.

FLOWERS

Strelitzias, proteas, orchids and many other exotic plants are grown on the "Island of Flowers" in nurseries where they can be purchased or ordered directly. Quality retailers (even small shops) will pack these fragile plants for safe transport at little or no additional cost. If you want to grow your own flowers, you'll find a wide variety of bulbs for sale in the market hall in Funchal.

BASKETRY

A new wicker armchair for your conservatory may be a little bulky to take home (although local retailers will send large items to your home address), but what about a pretty little bread basket from one of the basket weaver's studios in Camacha? The local cooperative Café Relógio offers all kinds of fancy items, in particular a whole army of heavy wooden frogs, finely decorated with willow twigs. You never know, one of them might be your Prince Charming?

MADEIRA EMBROIDERY

Political leaders as well as high-end fashionistas are in love with Madeira's authentic embroideries *(bordados)*. It was a British woman who turned the traditional stitchery of local fishermen's wives into a refined craft and a blossoming commercial endeavour. Nowadays, only a few professional

Madeira wine (left), embroidered hats (right)

bordadeiras are left. The prices for authentic *bordados* have skyrocketed as a result, which means that vendors are sometimes tempted to offer cheap, imported, machine-produced goods. When buying embroidery, check for the quality seal of the I.V.B.A.M. *(Instituto do Vinho, do Bordado e do Artesanato da Madeira).*

MADEIRA WINE

When buying Madeira wine, bear in mind the following rule of thumb: a good-quality wine has aged for at least five years. A fine old bottle of Madeira wine sometimes costs as much as the evening meal to go with it. However, the wine keeps for months or maybe years, even after it has been opened. At ⚑ *Blandy's Wine Lodge (Av. Arriaga 28 | Funchal | blandyswinelodge.com),* you can find out how Madeira wine is produced and taste and compare wines from different varieties of grapes and degrees of sweetness. And take your time …

PERFUME & COSMETICS

A scent from the island will bring a breath of fresh air to the cold winters of the northern hemisphere. The production of perfumes, particularly from orchids and strelitzias, and the manufacture of natural aloe vera cosmetics, count among Madeira's newest business ventures. Farmers can harvest the thick aloe leaves three times a year. The leaves are then pulverised and processed to manufacture cosmetics. The aloe plant can be turned into a wide range of products: shampoos, creams and ointments that soothe sunburn, torn muscles or arthritis. You can find them in well-stocked gift shops, some supermarkets, pharmacies and health-food stores.

INSIDER TIP
Aloe for body woe

SPORT & ACTIVITIES

Madeira is a paradise for hikers with its *levadas* and summit paths, but if you love water sports or are looking for a bit more action, you will discover a wide range of outdoor activities available here too.

CANYONING

Advanced-level hiking with a wetsuit, helmet and safety ropes; participants descend through canyons and over waterfalls. This adventure is a whole lot of fun and will give you a real adrenalin rush. Various operators organise canyoning, e.g. *Madeira Adventure Kingdom (mobile 968 101 870 | madeiraadventurekingdom. com)* and *Madeira Outdoor (mobile 966 230 212 | madeiraoutdoor.com)*.

DIVING

Exotic-looking species of fish abound in the often crystal-clear waters and delight divers as much as the bizarre underwater lava formations and caves. The diving stations are on the south and southeast coasts as well as on Porto Santo. The greatest diversity of sealife can be seen in the Garajau Marine National Park, which was established in 1986 to protect marine species. All diving stations offer taster sessions or courses in addition to their normal range of dives (from 29 euros).

INSIDER TIP
Close encounters with groupers

If you have some diving experience, you will love the shipwrecks: two off Porto Santo and one off Cabo Girão – the latter a decommissioned navy vessel that was sunk and now serves as an artificial reef. For information see e.g. *Manta Diving (in the Galoresort Hotel | Rua Robert Baden-Powell | Caniço de Baixo | tel. 291 935 588 | mantadiving.com); Madeira Divepoint (in the Carlton Hotel | Largo*

Mountain biker on the upland plain

António Nobre | Funchal | tel. 291 239 579 | madeiradivepoint.com).

HIKING

The best way to really get to know the landscape of Madeira is on foot – e.g. by doing a *levada* or mountain walk. Take care when planning a tour and bear in mind that the weather can change quickly, with fog and rain appearing or temperatures dropping suddenly. Don't forget to take a torch! There is water in some tunnels all year round, and others are unlit. More and more trails are being equipped with waymarkers, fences and hand-ropes, so that some hikes that used to present a fall risk are now safe. As the start and finish of a hike may be far apart, it is often useful to agree a pick-up point with a taxi driver in order to get back to base.

Organised tours are offered by, for example, *Madeira Explorers (Centro Comercial Estrada Monumental | Funchal | tel. 291 763 701 | mobile 962 797 887 | madeira-levada-walks. com/en)* or *Madeira Island Tours (Centro Comercial Estrada Monumental | Funchal | tel. 291 607 610 | madeiraislandtours.com)*.

Those who think that hiking is a little tame can go "trekking" or "trail running" at one of the numerous ultra-trail races where you cover many miles criss-crossing the mountains. The biggest event of its kind is the MIUT *(Madeira Island Ultra Trail, miutmadeira.com)* at the end of April, which sees athletes running up to 115km uphill and downhill across the entire island. You may feel your legs getting tired just from being an onlooker, but competitors love this race, and especially crossing the finish line in Machico.

MOUNTAIN BIKING

Steep climbs, breakneck descents, lonely mountain and forest tracks – what more could a cyclist want? You can hire bikes (mountain bikes and racing bikes) and book organised tours, for example at *Rainer Waschkewitz (Four Views Oasis Hotel | Caniço de Baixo | mobile 917 244 446 | madeira-bergziegen.de/en/enhome)*. The team of *BikeBus (mobile 927 096 376 | FB: BikeBusMadeira)* will also take you to the trails.

Even the Enduro bike scene has now discovered Madeira's *levadas* and mountain trails, although hikers and conservationists aren't at all happy about their encroachment on nature. For those who love racing down narrow steep tracks (ideally without crashing into the abyss or endangering hikers and the plant life), the guys at *Freeride (Rua Simplício Passos de Gouveia 21 | Funchal | mobile 925 977 046 | freeridemadeira.com)* offer guided day trips (incl. bike rental for 115 euros) and bike holidays.

Bicycling and mountain biking are pretty straightforward on Porto Santo because the mountains are not as high or as steep as those on Madeira, and there is little road traffic. Here, you can hire bicycles from 10 euros/day at e.g. *Auto Acessorios Colombo (Av. Viera de Castro 64 | Vila Baleira | tel. 291 984 438 | aacolombo.com)*.

PARAGLIDING

Run, run, run – then jump off the edge and take to the skies! Flights above the southwest coast, thermals permitting, can last for up to half an hour. Tandem flights are available with experienced paraglider Hartmut Peters. Provided that the weather is good, flying starts at approx. noon and may last until sunset. The starting point is the airbase in *Arco da Calheta (Rua da Achada de Santo Antão 212 | mobile 964 133 907 | madeira-paragliding.com)*.

Dolphin-spotting on a boat trip off the coast of Madeira

If you want to admire the stunning views on Madeira, you will need sturdy footwear

SAILING & BOAT TRIPS

You can go on a sailing excursion even if you do not have a sailing licence, either along the coast or to the Ilhas Desertas. Some trips include the opportunity to watch whales and dolphins, e. g. on board the *Bonita da Madeira (moors in Funchal marina | tel. 291 762 218 | bonitadamadeira.com)*. This two-masted ship – a 20-m wooden caravel built in 1996 – can accommodate up to 50 passengers for whale- and dolphin-watching trips on Wednesdays and Sundays, for a trip to the Ilhas Desertas on Tuesdays, Thursdays and Saturdays, and for a tour of Madeira's loveliest bays on Fridays.

STAND-UP PADDLEBOARDING

Beginners mostly start off on the southwest coast as the sea is normally calmer here. If you are an experienced paddle-boarder and would like to take to the waves on your SUP board, the organisers will find a suitable spot for you on the north coast. Courses and equipment are offered by companies such as *Around Freedom (mobile 961 874 993 | aroundfreedom.pt) or Madeira Outdoor (mobile 966 230 212 | madeiraoutdoor.com)*.

SURFING

The waves off the southwest coast of Madeira are a challenge for surfers. The coastal waters off Jardim do Mar and Paúl do Mar offer ideal conditions for experienced surfers. Anyone keen on learning how to surf can take lessons at the *Calhau Surf School (mobile 926 189 894 | madeira calhausurfschool.com)* or the *Madeira Surf Camp (mobile 962 903 118 | madeirasurfcamp. com)*. Both are based in Porto da Cruz, which has the best waves for beginners. Alternatively, you can hire boards and wetsuits and go surfing independently. For bodyboarding, we recommend *MadSea (mobile 966 107 010 | madsea.pt)*.

INSIDER TIP
Surf fun for beginners

REGIONAL OVERVIEW

OCEANO ATLÂNTICO

Porto Moniz

THE NORTH p. 72

Ponta do Pargo

Ribeira da Janela

São Vicente

THE SOUTHWEST p. 58

Calheta

Ponta do Sol

Ribeira Brava

Câmara de Lobos

For sun-lovers (and delicious fruit)

FUNCHAL p. 38

Pulsating island capital that loves its festivals

5 km
3.11 mi

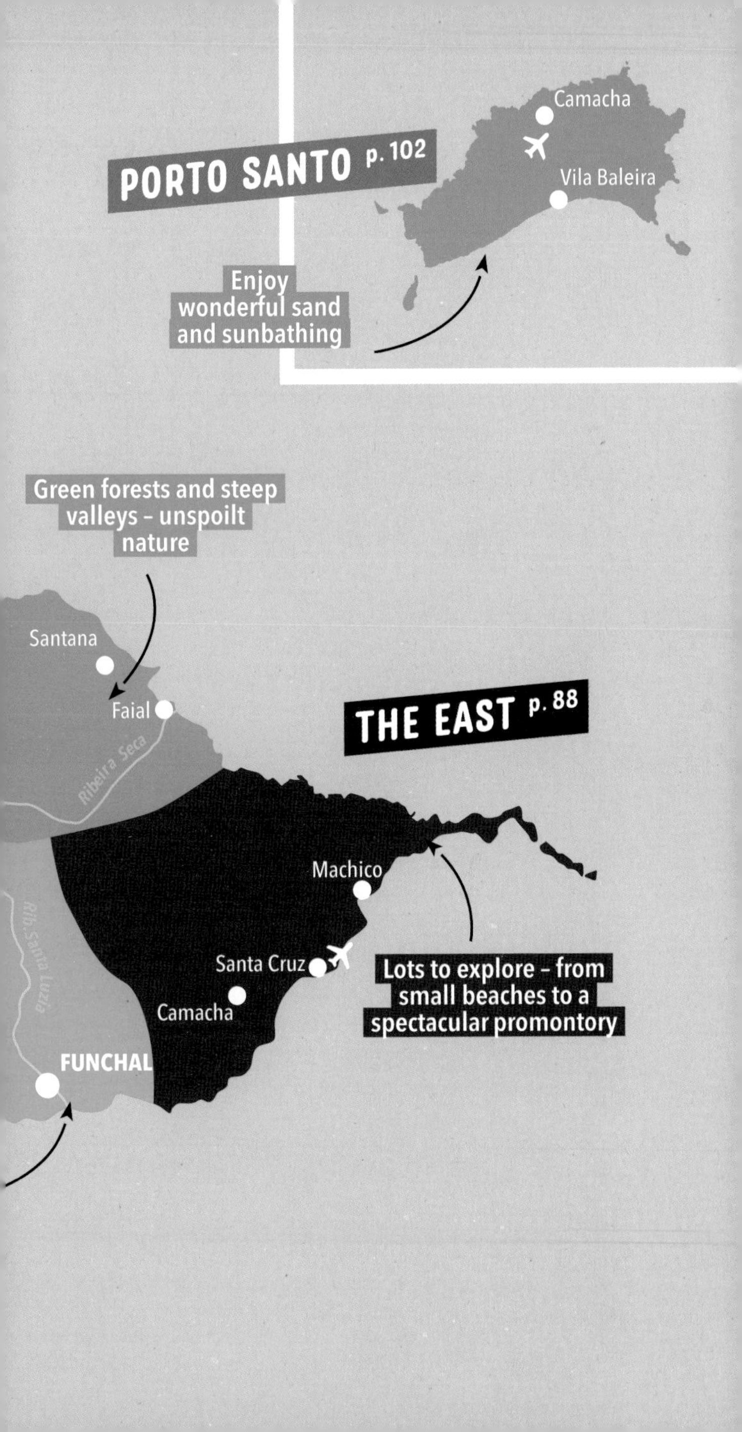

PORTO SANTO p. 102

Enjoy wonderful sand and sunbathing

Green forests and steep valleys – unspoilt nature

Santana

Faial

Ribeira Seca

THE EAST p. 88

Camacha

Vila Baleira

Machico

Rib. Santa Luzia

Santa Cruz

Lots to explore – from small beaches to a spectacular promontory

Camacha

FUNCHAL

FUNCHAL

CURTAIN UP FOR A BEAUTIFUL PERFORMANCE!

Several pretty churches, many small houses, a few grand *quintas* and countless hotels, all of them arranged in the rows of this "theatre" – the crescent-shaped bay with great sea views – as if they were waiting for the performance to begin.

Actually, it's the other way round: Funchal itself is the show. There is always something going on in the island's capital, and not just in the nightlife quarter of the old town. At any given time of year there's a festival celebrating something in Funchal: from the end of the year

The Monte Palace tropical garden in Funchal

(which starts in November!) to the Flower Festival (throughout the spring) to the music, Atlantic and wine festivals during the summer months. There is hardly a more beautiful sight than a firework display above the steep-sided bay where fennel once grew in abundance (*funcho* means plentiful fennel). And although Funchal is now home to more than 100,000 people, don't expect a concrete desert. Far from it! Funchal is steep but beautiful: its streets are clean, its front gardens are delightful and the parks are a dream.

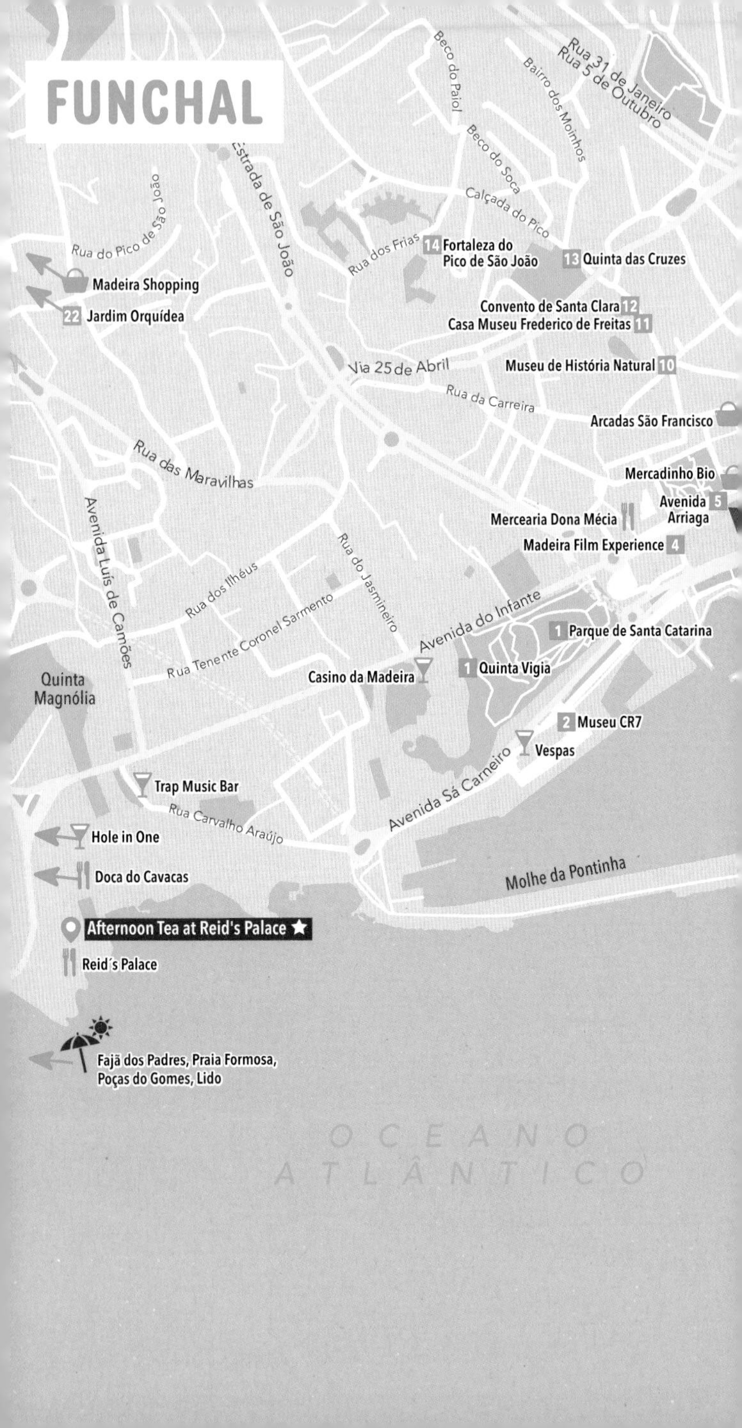

FUNCHAL

Rua 31 de Janeiro
Rua 5 de Outubro
Beco do Paiol
Beco do Soca
Bairro dos Moinhos
Calçada do Pico

Estrada de São João
Rua do Pico de São João

Rua dos Frias

14 Fortaleza do Pico de São João

13 Quinta das Cruzes

Convento de Santa Clara **12**
Casa Museu Frederico de Freitas **11**

Museu de História Natural **10**

Via 25 de Abril

Rua da Carreira

Arcadas São Francisco

Madeira Shopping

22 Jardim Orquídea

Mercadinho Bio

Avenida 5 Arriaga

Rua das Maravilhas

Mercearia Dona Mécia

Madeira Film Experience **4**

Avenida Luís de Camões

Rua dos Ilhéus

Rua do Jasmineiro

Rua Tenente Coronel Sarmento

Avenida do Infante

1 Parque de Santa Catarina

Casino da Madeira

1 Quinta Vigia

Quinta Magnólia

2 Museu CR7

Vespas

Avenida Sá Carneiro

Trap Music Bar

Rua Carvalho Araújo

Molhe da Pontinha

Hole in One

Doca do Cavacas

Afternoon Tea at Reid's Palace ★

Reid's Palace

Fajã dos Padres, Praia Formosa, Poças do Gomes, Lido

OCEANO
ATLÂNTICO

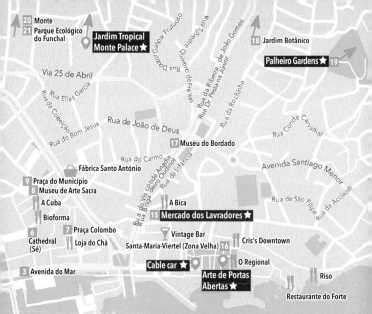

20 Monte
21 Parque Ecológico do Funchal

Jardim Tropical Monte Palace ★

18 Jardim Botânico

Palheiro Gardens ★ 19

Via 25 de Abril

Rua Elias Garcia
Rua da Conceição
Rua do Bom Jesus
Rua de João de Deus

Rua Dolorosa
Rua Gaspar Frutuoso
Quinta de Freitas
Rua do Silvestre
Rua da Ribeira de João Gomes
Rua Dr Pestana na Junior
Rua da Rochinha

Rua Conde Carvalhal

Avenida Santiago Menor

17 Museu do Bordado

Rua do Carmo
Fábrica Santo António

Rua do Visconde Anadia
Rua Brigadeiro Oudinot
Rua da Infância

Rua de São Filipe
Rua de Acciaoli

9 Praça do Município
8 Museu de Arte Sacra
A Cuba
Bioforma

A Bica

15 Mercado dos Lavradores ★

Rua de São Filipe

Cris's Downtown

6 Cathedral (Sé)
7 Praça Colombo
Loja do Chá

Vintage Bar
Santa-Maria-Viertel (Zona Velha) 16

O Regional

3 Avenida do Mar

Cable car ★

Arte de Portas Abertas ★

Riso

Restaurante do Forte

Bahia de Funchal

MARCO POLO HIGHLIGHTS

★ **MERCADO DOS LAVRADORES**
The market halls are a treat for the eye, nose and palate ➤ p. 46

★ **ARTE DE PORTAS ABERTAS**
Admire colourful doors in the lanes of the Old Town, Funchal's nightlife quarter ➤ p. 47

★ **CABLE CAR**
Take a trip over the roofs of Funchal to Monte ➤ p. 47

★ **PALHEIRO GARDENS**
A landscaped garden with colourful blossom and an English touch ➤ p. 48

★ **JARDIM TROPICAL MONTE PALACE**
Dream-like landscaped park with a fairy-tale atmosphere ➤ p. 50

★ **AFTERNOON TEA AT REID'S PALACE**
Enjoy scones and cakes on the legendary terrace of this luxury hotel ➤ p. 52

200 m
219 yd

FUNCHAL

(📖 K–M 7–8) **In Funchal you can wander to your heart's content: along the seaside promenade on the Atlantic, under the jacaranda trees in the Avenida Arriaga, down the colourful back streets in the old town and through the magnificent municipal gardens.**

You can easily explore the historical city centre and the spruced-up fishermen's quarter *(Zona Velha)* on foot, and scheduled bus services and cable cars take you to the parks and gardens which are slightly outside the city centre. If you prefer to be driven around, the commented tour (1½ hours, also in English) on the open-top double-decker bus *(Yellowbus | from 12.60 euros | hopon hopoff ticket valid for 24 hrs | departure point: Avenida do Mar,* *above the marina | yellowbustours. com)* will give you an initial impression. However, if you want to explore Funchal in more detail, you should plan to spend at least two days here.

▮ PARQUE DE SANTA CATARINA & QUINTA VIGIA

You can go for wonderful walks in *St Catherine's Park* with its exotic trees, colourful flower beds, 15th-century Baroque chapel and fantastic views over the harbour. It's great for people-watching too. At the upper end of the elongated park, the rose-coloured walls of the *Quinta Vigia* are just about visible through dense and sumptuous vegetation. Today, this historic mansion built in the 17th century is the official residence and guesthouse of the president of the regional

Afternoon stroll along the Avenida Arriaga

government. You really should visit the park with its aviaries *(Mon–Fri | admission 1 euro)* that is attached to the Quinta. A little further towards the hotel area, a bronze statue of "Sisi" commemorates the sojourn in 1860/61 of the Austrian Empress Elisabeth; today the casino designed by Oscar Niemeyer is located on this spot.

WHERE TO START?

Old town: With its narrow lanes, the old town of Funchal *(Zona Velha)* is a good place to start a visit. At the western edge of the old town, you can park in the Almirante Reis multi-storey car park *(Rua Dom Carlos I)*. The central bus station and terminus of the cable car to Monte are also here. The market hall *(Mercado dos Lavradores)* and the São Tiago fortress are close by and it is only a few minutes to the city centre and marina.

2 MUSEU CR7 ☂

Die-hard Ronaldo fans come to Madeira to discover the home ground of Portugal's most famous football star. But a visit to the museum is also worthwhile for sceptics or secret admirers. Ronaldo's life story and road to success are impressively presented; alongside many other trophies, you can see his "Golden Balls". *Mon–Sat 10am–6pm | admission 5 euros | Av. Sá Cameiro | Praça do Mar 27 | museucr7.com | ⏱ 1½ hrs*

3 AVENIDA DO MAR

The seafront promenade in Funchal has been the site of substantial rebuilding in recent years: in 2010, severe storms caused more than a square kilometre of rubble to fall into the sea and the "reclaimed land" was transformed into a new cruise-ship mooring place and the *Praça do Povo* park. Parallel to the main road with its many bus stops, you can now walk alongside the water's edge, enjoy people-watching in one of the cafés or gaze at the giant cruise ships leaving the harbour. The imposing *Fortaleza de São Lourenço* is situated on the other side of the street and is now a government building. The island's parliament meets next door in the hemispherical structure, which is the former customs house, the *Alfândega Velha*.

4 MADEIRA FILM EXPERIENCE 😷

In this cinema, a sophisticated documentary tells you all there is to know about Madeira's history in half an hour, and headphones provide an English voice-over. *Screenings daily every 45 mins between 10.15am and 5pm | admission 5 euros, ☛ children up to 12 free | Marina Shopping loja 223 | Rua Conselheiro José Silvestre | madeirafilmexperience.com*

5 AVENIDA ARRIAGA

The elegant promenade runs from the cathedral to the *Praça do Infante* with the monument to Henry the Navigator. When the jacaranda trees are in bloom in late spring, you feel as if you are walking beneath a lilac canopy. You pass through the Neoclassical Municipal Theatre *Teatro Municipal Baltazar Dias*, built at the beginning of the 20th century, and the legendary *Ritz Café (theritzmadeira.com)* whose elegant façade tells stories from the island in blue and white *azulejo* tiles. Opposite is the almost tropical *Jardim Municipal* with its fragrant frangipani and an impressive sausage tree *(Kigelia)*. This was formerly the site of the garden belonging to the Franciscan monastery where today you can taste and purchase the famous Madeira wine made by the Blandy vintner family: *Blandy's Wine Lodge (tours in English Mon–Fri 10.45am, 2.45pm and 3.45pm, Sat 10.45am | 45-min tour with wine tasting 5.90 euros | Av. Arriaga 28 | blandyswinelodge.com).*

⑥ CATHEDRAL (SÉ)

King Manuel I ordered the construction of Funchal's leading place of worship. The church was completed between 1485 and 1514, and is one of the city's few surviving examples of Manueline architecture. Its steeple is clad in multi-coloured roof tiles, while in the plain stone-built façade a majestic Gothic doorway catches the eye. The architecture at the eastern end of the church with the apse is more playful: turrets twist like screws, and the balustrade is elaborately decorated. The finest feature inside is the 16th-century wooden roof in Mudéjar style, which is inlaid with ivory. It is arguably the best example of its kind in the whole of Portugal.

The best place to get a good view of the cathedral is from the Rua da Sé. *Opening hours Mon–Fri 9am–noon and 4–5.30pm, Sat 4.15–5.30pm, Sun 10–11am and 4.15–5pm | admission free | Largo da Sé*

⑦ PRAÇA COLOMBO

What does Columbus Square have to do with the famous seafarer? Not a lot, as he probably only spent a few days here to conduct some business in 'sugar town'. During the 15th and 16th centuries, the 'white gold' triggered a boom on Madeira: this explains why the city's coat of arms created as a mosaic at the centre of the attractively renovated square contains five sugar loaves. In the ☛ *Museu Cidade do Açucar (Closed Sat/Sun | admission free | Praça de Colombo 5)* you can learn interesting facts about the history of the sugar trade. The palatial mansion belonging to the Flemish sugar merchant João Esmeraldo (actually called Jean d'Esmenault) once stood here. The museum displays archaeological finds including ceramic moulds for sugar loaves.

⑧ MUSEU DE ARTE SACRA

You can admire a unique collection of Flemish paintings in this Museum of Religious Art. The paintings came to Madeira during the 16th century when the sugar barons were paid for their precious commodity with works of art. *Closed Sat afternoon and Sun | admission 5 euros | Rua do Bispo 21 | masf.pt*

The inner courtyard of Funchal's city hall is an oasis of tranquillity

🟨 PRAÇA DO MUNICÍPIO

Standing on the square with its black-and-white cobblestones you can see three of Funchal's significant historic buildings. At the end of the square is the former town residence of the Counts of Carvalhal. Since the late 19th century this Baroque palace with its magnificent, *azulejo*-adorned courtyard has been the home of the *city hall*. The northwest side of the square is dominated by what used to be a Jesuit college and is now the *University of Madeira* with an impressive church, the *Igreja do Colégio*. Opposite the church, the Bishop's Palace now houses the Museum of Religious Art (see above). University students run ➤ *Quick Tours (Mon–Fri 10am–4pm | 12.90*

INSIDER TIP
Uni quick tour

euros | colegiodosjesuitas.pt | ⏱ 2 hrs) through the buildings of the Jesuit college which are steeped in history. Register in their *Gaudeamos* shop (which also sells lovely souvenirs) in the Rua dos Ferreiros.

🔟 MUSEU DE HISTÓRIA NATURAL
👣 🐾

Funchal's municipal museum is somewhat old school and perhaps a little fusty but is really not bad if you want to find out more about Madeira's flora and fauna or need somewhere to go to brighten up a rainy day. What is more, the aquariums provide an impression of the archipelago's marine world. *Closed Mon | admission adults 3.91 euros, children (11–17) 1.91 euros, ➤ Sundays free | Rua da Mouraria 31 | ⏱ 1½ hrs*

11 CASA MUSEU FREDERICO DE FREITAS

This 17th-century villa is filled with valuable furniture, old *azulejos*, religious and Chinese art. Its former owner also collected drawn and painted views of his Madeiran homeland. *Closed Sun/Mon | admission 3 euros | Calçada de Santa Clara 7 | casamuseuff.blogspot.com*

12 CONVENTO DE SANTA CLARA

If you want to visit the convent which houses a cornucopia of art treasures, you first have to ring the bell and wait until one of the nuns opens the door. When the convent was built in the late 15th century, it was inhabited by the Poor Clares, but now it's one of the Franciscan nuns (who have lived here since 1896 and run a nursery school in the old buildings) who will let you in. She will show you the special altars and chapels, the cloisters and the interior of the church whose walls are completely tiled with *azulejos* dating from the 17th century. The church also houses the graves of the two daughters of Zarco, the man who "discovered" the island. It's possible that Zarco himself is buried there too. *Closed Sun | admission 2 euros | Calçada de Santa Clara 15*

13 QUINTA DAS CRUZES

The home of João Zarco is said to have occupied this site. However, today's residence dates from the 18th century and is a museum where you can get to know the lifestyle of wealthy citizens of Madeira in the past. The *quinta* lies within an archaeological park with exotic plants and stone Manueline windows, as well as a fragment of the 15th-century pillory *(pelourinho)* of Funchal. *Closed Mon | admission 3 euros, 🐷 Sun and garden free | Calçada do Pico 1 | mqc.madeira.gov.pt*

14 FORTALEZA DO PICO DE SÃO JOÃO

High up on the 111-m-high Pico dos Frias, this fort, which was built early in the 17th century under Spanish rule, commands one of the best views of the city centre of Funchal. The historic walls also feature a nice café, the *A Janela do Forte*, as well as a small exhibition on the history of the fort. *Daily 10am-6.30pm | Rua do Castelo*

15 MERCADO DOS LAVRADORES ★

The art deco market hall built in 1940 is a festival for the senses! It smells of flowers and fruit (apart from the fish hall, obviously) and the colourful fruit stalls and scary-looking scabbard fish are crying out to be photographed. Many of the fruit stallholders are only too keen to offer you tasty samples of passion fruit or other exotic delicacies to tempt you to buy these expensive fruits.

On Fridays, the courtyard is full of farmers offering their fresh vegetables for sale. If you would prefer to escape the crowds, there is a welcoming café with comfortable wicker furniture on the roof terrace above the fish hall. *Mon-Thu 8am-7pm, Fri 7am-8pm, Sat 7am-2pm | Rua Latino Coelho*

From cabbages to potatoes: Madeira's vegetables on show at the Mercado dos Lavradores

16 SANTA MARIA DISTRICT (ZONA VELHA)

You will be charmed by Funchal's old town. In recent years, the formerly dilapidated fishermen's quarter has been converted into a fashionable nightlife destination with numerous bars, restaurants and *fado* houses. A special attraction are the brightly painted doors in the district which have been designed by local artists, thanks to the art project ★ *artE depORtas abErtas (arteportasabertas. com)*. In contrast, if you ascend to Monte with the ★ cable car *Teleféricos da Madeira (daily 9am–5.45pm | 11 euros, return ticket 16 euros) | madeira cablecar.com)*, you will notice that several 18th- and 19th-century buildings are still awaiting restoration. Despite a great deal of refurbishment, the narrow streets still exude an impression of the original atmosphere: you can still find quaint little

corner shops and traditional craft workshops alongside the trendy boutiques.

The *Capela do Corpo Santo*, a brotherhood chapel built by fishermen and dating from the Manueline period, is situated in the middle of this quarter. On the eastern edge of the old town, you should not miss the pure Baroque façade of the *Igreja do Socorro* dating from the 18th century. Opposite this building, a lift takes you down to the coastal bathing complex *Barreirinha*.

The most striking building in the Zona Velha is the yellow-painted *Forte de São Tiago*, which was constructed as a defence against pirates from 1614 onwards: there are plans to house Madeira's archaeological museum collection there in the near future. While on the subject of museums, if you are interested in the history of the island, and especially when travelling with children, you should certainly go on a journey through time in the interactive 👥 *Madeira Story Centre (daily 9am–7pm | admission adults 5 euros, children 3 euros | Rua D Carlos I 27 | madeira storycentre.com | ⏱ 1½ hrs)*, where there is a lot to see, ranging from the volcanic origins of the island to the archipelago's significant historical events. What's more,

INSIDER TIP
A history lesson from the top

you have an amazing view of the old town from the highly recommended roof garden restaurant on the third floor!

In the 👥 electricity museum, *Casa da Luz (Tue–Sat 10am–12.30pm and 2–6pm | admission adults 2.70 euros, children (from age 12) 1.35 euros | Rua Casa da Luz 2 | eem.pt | ⏱ 1 hr)* in the former thermal power station, children can generate electricity themselves. And in the 👥 *Museu do Brinquedo (Mon–Sat 10am–6pm | admission adults 5 euros, children 3 euros | Rua Latino Coelho 39 | FB: museudobrinquedo | ⏱ 1 hr)* even grown-ups will feel nostalgic when faced with the more than 20,000 toys.

17 MUSEU DO BORDADO

This is certainly anything but a stuffy location! In the Embroidery Museum, housed in the State Institute for Wine, Embroidery and Applied Arts (I.V.B.A.M.), you can admire the stylishly embroidered objects dating from the 19th century and the Art Nouveau period, presented alongside tapestries. *Closed Sat/Sun | admission 2 euros | Rua Visconde de Anadia 44 | FB: bordadomadeiraembroidery*

18 JARDIM BOTÂNICO 🚩

There is always something in bloom in the Botanical Garden thanks to the hard-working gardeners and the favourable climate. During your tour round the different sections of the garden situated about 3km from the city centre, you will gain a vivid impression of the tropical, subtropical and native plants that flourish on Madeira. In the 19th century, the *Quinta do Bom Sucesso* ("of good success") with its approximately 20 acres of land belonged to the hotelier family Reid: the first trees were actually planted during this period. Today, the old manor house presents a touchingly old-fashioned natural history exhibition. A small *terrace café* is hidden among the luscious greenery near the *miradouro*. The valley station of the *cable car (daily 9am–5pm | 8.25 euros, return ticket 12.75 euros | teleferico jardimbotanico.com)*, spanning the *Ribeira de João Gomes* gorge and leading to Monte, is situated at the northern edge of the park. *Jardim Botânico: daily 9am–6pm, in summer until 7pm | admission 6 euros | Caminho do Meio.*

19 PALHEIRO GARDENS ⭐

On the old road to Camacha, 9km east of Funchal at 600m above sea level, you can find one of the island's most beautiful and varied gardens: the Palheiro Gardens.

The *Quinta do Palheiro Ferreiro* once belonged to the Count of Carvalhal. In the 18th century, he used this grand house as a hunting lodge, but his descendants wasted away the family fortune. As a result, in 1885 the estate became the country seat of the Blandy family, a British dynasty of wine merchants. They built themselves a new residence in the grounds. This private country villa is surrounded by a carefully planned English garden with superb subtropical plants in the Sunken Garden, the Long Border and the cosy Tea House. There is no other park on the island with such skilful topiary in the shape of box turkeys, fabulous camellias and exquisite protea blossom. *Daily 9am–5.30pm | admission 11 euros | palheirogardens.com*

⑳ MONTE

Up in Monte, the climate is generally slightly cooler and damper. During the 18th and 19th centuries, numerous elegant manor houses were built on the slope 8km above Funchal, many of which were inhabited by wealthy Britons and the high society from other European countries. In 1921, Karl I, the last Austrian Emperor, sought refuge in exile here and accepted the offer to stay with an acquainted family. It was probably the damp lodgings that brought on the bout of pneumonia that would be the cause of his death a year later. The now-beatified Habsburg monarch is buried in the pilgrim church *Nossa Senhora do Monte*. In the main square below the church – the idyllic *Largo da Fonte* with the former valley station of the cog railway which was in operation between 1894 and 1943 – the inhabitants of the island come to fetch healing water from a spring. The pretty ☛ *Municipal Garden (admission free)* stretches from here down to the valley along the ramp of the former cog railway.

In front of the church steps, the drivers of the ⚑ *basket sledges (Mon–Sat 9am–6pm | 30 euros for a double*

The cable car to Monte is only recommended if you have a head for heights

Reid's Palace still conveys a British colonial atmosphere

sledge | carreirosdomonte.com) are waiting to steer their customers in these historical sledges *(carros de cestos)* approx. 2km down to Livramento where expensive taxis are on standby. This sledge ride without snow and in between the moving traffic is probably unique in the world and therefore a special highlight for tourists.

Equally spectacular is the 15-minute ride in the modern *cabin cable car* departing from the station next to the Tropical Palace Garden in Monte. In 1987, the wealthy South African José Berardo ("Joe Gold") bought the overgrown property where he created the enchanting artistic and tropical garden ★ *Jardim Tropical Monte Palace (daily 9.30am–6pm | admission 12.50 euros | Caminho do Monte 174 | montepalace.com)*. You can stroll among a fairy-tale jumble of laurel trees, palm ferns, *azulejo* tiles, terracotta soldiers and other artworks,

walking past koi fishponds, Buddha figurines and oriental doorways. You can also marvel at the largest vase in the world made on a potter's wheel at the romantic swan lake. Do not forget to visit the *Monte Palace Museum* in the upper part of the garden: more than 1,000 sculptures from Zimbabwe are exhibited on the top two floors and one of the largest private mineral collections can be found in the basement: the exhibition "Mother Nature's Secrets" displays an astonishing array of glittering precious stones and minerals.

INSIDER TIP
Sparkling natural treasures

ᴎ PARQUE ECOLÓGICO DO FUNCHAL

Between Monte, the Pico do Arieiro, the Poiso Pass and Camacha is a protected area of around 8km² chiefly devoted to reforestation projects following forest fires. This is of great importance to Funchal because heavy rainfall uphill has resulted in the city being flooded several times in the past. The soil therefore needs to be protected against erosion. The *Centro de Recepção e Interpretação (Mon-Fri 9am-5pm | Estrada Regional 103, No. 259)* displays information charts on flora and fauna and offers workshops and environmental educational courses for school classes and other interested groups. Several hiking paths cross the nature reserve, and information is available in the visitor centre, for example about the *Poço da Neve* (snow well) in the area's upper part. This construction was once used to store snow which then turned into ice and, in summer, was used for making sorbet in the Reid's Palace.

⯒ JARDIM ORQUÍDEA

During the devastating forest fires of 2016, the Austrian Pregetter family of orchid growers lost their show garden, lovingly created over decades, to the flames. With great effort another garden is now being planted at a new site in the Santo António district. Despite many of the plants being in their infancy, head gardener Verena is always pleased to show plant-lovers her little treasures and the progress of the work. Her wild paradise, which resembles a phoenix rising from the ashes, holds many botanical surprises. *Visits only by appointment | admission on a donation basis | Beco do Jacinto 1 | Santo António | mobile 916 770 251*

A BICA

Have the courage to go down the inconspicuous steps. In this cosy restaurant next to the market hall, you can mingle with the locals, eat good food at reasonable prices and take a look at the nostalgic photos of Funchal on the walls. *Closed on Sun | Rua Hospital Velho 17 | tel. 291 221 346 | €*

A CUBA

On first sight, this snug *adega* looks like a wine bodega: there are even a few tables standing inside a gigantic wine barrel. However, the rustic atmosphere is only part of the allure. Here you can try Madeira's typical specialities, such as tomato soup, scabbard fish, *bolo do caco* or meat skewers. The excellent pepper steak is also recommended. Despite its central location, the prices are unbeatably modest, particularly if you order a dish of the day for lunch. *Closed on Sun | Rua do Bispo 28 | tel. 291 646 930 | €€*

BIOFORMA

A highlight for vegetarians even though the snack bar is on the lower floor of an organic grocery store and only serves lunch. However, the dishes are tasty and good value. *Closed Sat/Sun | Rua da Queimada de Cima 31 | tel. 291 229 262 | bioformaonline. com | €*

CRIS'S DOWNTOWN

The popular restaurants owned by Cris's family are record-breaking in many ways, and that's unsurprising given the excellent cuisine, great service and stylish locations. Now they have a new branch in the old town. The gourmet menus are true culinary journeys of exploration of the island. *Rua de Santa Maria 141 | tel. 291 221 707 | €€€*

DOCA DO CAVACAS
A fish restaurant by the sea – just the way it's supposed to be, and particularly romantic at sunset. The *Poças do Gomes* natural swimming pools located below the restaurant are also worth a visit. *Rua Ponta Cruz | Estrada Monumental | tel. 291 762 057 | FB: rdocadocavacas | €€*

LOJA DO CHÁ 🎋
The tea house in Funchal: in this inviting café, you can not only meet for tea, but also for tasty scones and snacks. Enjoy the hustle and bustle on the esplanade or the cosy living-room flair inside. *Rua do Sabão 33-35 | tel. 291 221 309 | lojadochamadeira.com | €*

MERCEARIA DONA MÉCIA
With its delicious daily specials and cakes, this small terrace café located in the inner courtyard of an old-fashioned-style grocery shop in the city centre is a local institution. *Closed Sun | Rua dos Aranhas 26 | tel. 291 221 559 | FB: Mercearia.Dona.Mecia | €*

O REGIONAL

INSIDER TIP
Spaghetti and stew

From the garlic bread with home-made dips to the more-than-delicious *Esparguete de Marisco* (a seafood stew with spaghetti), the dishes served here delight the palate, and the waiters with their traditional colourful waistcoats are helpful and friendly. *Rua de Dom Carlos I 54 | tel. 291 232 956 | restauranteoregionalfunchal. com | €€*

REID'S PALACE
The best and most venerable hotel in town also serves food: the gourmet restaurant *William (Tue–Sat 7.30–10pm | €€€)* has a Michelin star. Absolutely legendary is their ★ *Afternoon Tea (daily 3–4.30pm | €€€)* on the picturesque terrace: you drink your tea, which is served by a spotlessly presented butler, let your eye wander across the fantastic garden to the Atlantic and enjoy beautiful scones and delicious cakes. *Estrada Monumental 139 | tel. 291 717 030 (you will need to book a table 1–2 days in advance!) | belmond.com*

RESTAURANTE DO FORTE
Are you looking for somewhere elegant to have dinner? In the tent pavilion in the São Tiago fortress, local dishes such as scabbard fish are imaginatively interpreted and, should you wish, you can be driven there in a vintage car. *Rua Portão São Tiago | tel. 291 215 580 | forte.restaurant | €€€*

RISO
Here, everything revolves around rice. Portuguese classics are combined with the tastes of Asia and are served in imaginative variations from crispy to sweet. If the weather is fine, you can sit on a wonderful terrace on the cliffs.

Rua de Santa Maria 274 | tel. 291 280 360 | riso-fx.com | €€

SHOPPING

MADEIRA SHOPPING

The largest shopping mall on Madeira is situated above Funchal with over 100 shops, a cinema, almost 20 restaurants and cafés and a *hipermercado* – ideal for a rainy day. *Caminho de Santa Quitéria 45 | Santo António | madeirashopping.pt*

MERCADINHO BIO

Every Wednesday, Madeira's organic farmers sell their produce on the *Av. Arriaga*.

FÁBRICA SANTO ANTÓNIO

You can find home-made confectionery, jams, sorbets and biscuits in this historic shop. *Travessa do Forno 27–29*

SÃO FRANCISCO

In the centre of Funchal, there are several nice shopping arcades. The small shopping centre located in the grounds of the former Franciscan monastery is particularly attractive with boutiques, a flower shop and cafés. In the neighbouring *Blandy's Wine Lodge* (see p. 31) you can taste and buy Madeira wine. *Closed Sun | Rua São Francisco 20 | arcadassao francisco.pt*

SPORT & ACTIVITIES

The *Promenade do Lido* stretches for 7km from the public swimming pool to Câmara de Lobos along the seafront

Santa Maria de Colombo

promenade and is ideal for walking and burning off those excess calories.

**INSIDER TIP
Along the seafront**

Children (and their parents!) are mesmerised by the Santa Maria de Colombo (daily 10.30am and 3pm, 3-hr trip | admission adults 35 euros, children 17.50 euros | santamaria decolombo.com), a replica of the sailing ship that took Columbus to the New World. It is moored next to the Praça do Povo. The crew are dressed up as pirates and steer the passengers to Cabo Girão, and with a bit of luck you will be escorted by dolphins.

BEACHES

Funchal does not have a sandy beach for sunbathers as in Calheta and Machico, but there are some attractive ways to get into the sea – via steps on the rocky coast or across the pebbles of a beach. 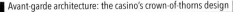 *Praia Formosa* in the west of Funchal, much loved by young locals, is one such pebbly beach. Tennis courts, restaurants and bars round off the fun. In Funchal's hotel district on the promenade, there are two secure pools that charge for admission (*Lido and Ponta Gorda, 5 euros each*). In addition to steps leading down to the sea, they have proper swimming pools, paddling pools for children, slides spaces for sunbathing and sanitary facilities. The natural tidal pool *Poças do Gomes (2 euros)*, situated between Praia Formosa and the western end of the promenade, is somewhat smaller, cheaper and has no man-made pool. In the historic quarter opposite the Igreja do Socorro, the *Barreirinha* pool charges 2 euros while a little pebble beach next to the São Tiago fort costs nothing and is popular with local children.

WELLNESS

Funchal has numerous hotels with spas and most of them are open to non-residents who are looking to treat themselves to a wellness day. Particularly elegant facilities can be found in *The Vine Hotel (daily 11am–7pm | massage incl. Madeira wine 75 euros/50 mins | Rua das Aranhas 27 | tel. 291 009 000 | hotelthevine.com)*. You may use the spa facilities before and after booked treatments.

NIGHTLIFE

There is always something going on in Funchal: particularly at the weekend,

Avant-garde architecture: the casino's crown-of-thorns design

the *poncha* bars and *fado* houses in the old town (Zona Velha) are full in the evening as well as the (rooftop) bars and pubs on the promenade in the Lido district and near the Pestana Carlton Hotel focused around the Rua Favila. Some cafés are even transformed into popular music bars, e.g. the *Café do Teatro (Sun–Thu 8am–1am, Fri 10am–4am, Sat 9am–5am | Av. Arriaga | FB: cafedoteatro)* next to the city's theatre. After midnight, the clubs begin welcoming customers (the admission price frequently includes a drink) with DJ sets and live acts. Dancing to Afro and Latin rhythms is especially popular on Madeira.

CASINO DA MADEIRA

Diners and clubbers, gamblers and architecture aficionados all rave about the casino. This extravagant construction was designed by Brazilian cult architect Oscar Niemeyer in the shape of a crown of thorns that resembles the cathedral of Brasília. Night owls come to try their luck at the gaming tables and dance to live music in the *Discoteca Copacabana. Av. do Infante | casinodamadeira.com*

HOLE IN ONE

This café with its cosy outdoor seating area turns into a trendy music bar in the evening. The live performances by Portuguese and international musicians will delight a wide audience and not just the golfing crowd. *Daily 11am–2am | Estrada Monumental 238a*

TRAP MUSIC BAR

This lounge bar and disco in the hotel quarter is glitzy and glamourous. Live bands perform at weekends and the dancing goes on until the early hours. *Mon–Thu 8pm–4am, Fri/Sat 8pm–5am | Rua do Favilla 7 | FB: TRAPPUB*

VESPAS

On weekends and before public holidays, this traditional disco at the cruise ship harbour plays house, electro and pop music for its youthful crowd. Women have free admission and can enjoy a drink on the house on the regularly held 🐖 "Ladies Nights". *Fri/Sat midnight–7am | Av. Sá Carneiro 7 | FB: VespasClub*

VINTAGE BAR

In this popular bar in the Zona Velha, the spirit of the 1970s, 1980s and 1990s lives on. Accordingly, it's a favourite night spot for the over-30 crowd. *Tue–Thu, Sun 5pm–1am, Fri/Sat 8pm–3am | Rua Santa Maria 23 | FB: 23VintageBar*

AROUND FUNCHAL

🗺 CURRAL DAS FREIRAS
15km / 30 mins by car via the ER107
A trip to the "valley of the nuns" is literally breathtaking, particularly if you happen to meet a bus coming from the opposite direction on the drive up the narrow mountain road to the viewpoint *Eira do Serrado* (1,095m). However, the thrilling drive is worth taking: the view from the

miradouro of the "valley of the nuns", about 500m below, and the jagged mountain tops surrounding the almost circular valley basin is astounding. The valley was formerly thought to be the crater of a volcano, although the landscape was actually created by the stream which snakes through the ravine. There is no convent here, although the name of the town – which translates as "stable of the nuns" – originates from the sisters of the Poor Clares in the Convent St Clare in Funchal who owned land (and stables) here. The original chapel erected by the nuns has now been replaced with a modern building.

From the cemetery, you have a grand view across the lower part of the valley and the steep rock face on which an amazing hiking trail (approx. 1½ hours) with old paving ascends to *Eira do Serrado*. Specialities from the valley are available in the rural taverns: sweet chestnuts in all variations. An especially good place to sit is on the terrace of the *Sabores do Curral* (*Caminho da Pedra | tel. 291 712 257 | €*). ⌘ *J5–6*

INSIDER TIP
Serpentine trail up the rock face

24 CÂMARA DE LOBOS
9km / 20 mins by car via the Estrada Monumental

Câmara de Lobos (pop. 18,000) takes its name from the monk seals (*Lobos marinhos*) living here at the time of Madeira's discovery. Several years ago the town had gained the reputation of having the most serious social problems (unemployment, alcohol and drugs) on the island. However, today you can take a wonderful stroll along the coast and through the old town. Particularly attractive is the walking and jogging path towards Funchal that goes past the swimming pool and along the seafront.

The town is located in a picturesque narrow bay where colourfully painted fishing boats are jacked up and sometimes dried fish can be seen hanging in the sun, offering numerous photo opportunities. Winston Churchill was a great fan of this idyllic harbour, which he painted from a small panoramic terrace west of the harbour during his stay on Madeira in 1949/50. A plaque commemorates the artistically gifted politician.

In the fishermen's quarter, it is well worth visiting the *Capela de Nossa Senhora da Conceição*. The chapel was built on the personal order of Zarco, the discoverer of the island, when the town was established in the 15th century and was later reconstructed by the charitable brotherhood of the fishermen. The interior features paintings depicting fishing scenes.

After walking past numerous pubs and bars, you will come to the parish church *São Sebastião*. It is decorated with blue and yellow Baroque tiles and concealed behind a striking cliff. Behind it is the newly renovated square *Largo da República*.

The light-flooded restaurant *Vila do Peixe* (*Rua Doutor João Abel de Freitas 30 | tel. 291 099 909 | viladopeixe.com | €€*) offers excellent fresh fish cooked on the grill. | ⌘ *J8*

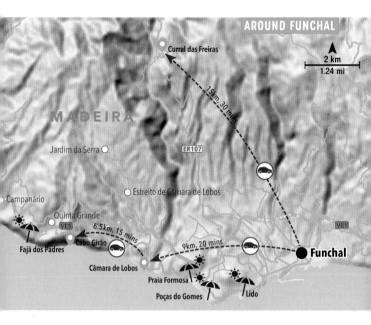

25 CABO GIRÃO

14km / 20 mins by car via the Via Rápida

There is a spectacular, steep, 580-m drop at the so-called "Cape of Return", where only the glass platform of the Skywalk stands between you and the coast several hundred metres below. The view is breathtaking – provided you don't suffer from vertigo. On clear days, you can see as far as Funchal in the east.

On the coast below, wine and vegetables are cultivated on the narrow, fertile alluvial strip of land known as *Fajã do Gabo Girão*. If you would like to explore this area, you have to take the *cable car (5 euros)* in the district of Rancho, slightly east of Cabo Girão: this is also how the farmers access their fields on the seashore. Down there you will feel as if you are on a desert island. ⌑ H8

26 FAJÃ DOS PADRES 🌴

13km / 15 mins by car via the VR1

Madeira's newest cable car descends 300m to the *Fajã dos Padres* in four minutes – a breathtaking experience. At the bottom, a paradise awaits you where you can take a stroll through pergolas covered in grape vines, snorkel in the jetty area and bathe in the crystal-clear water by the pebble beach. We recommend the Caribbean-style *restaurant (tel. 291 944 538 | €€)*. *Cablecar Fajã dos Padres (Rua Padre António Dinis Henriques | Quinta Grande | daily 11am–6pm; in summer Mon–Thu 10am–6pm, Fri–Sun 10am–7pm | return ticket 10 euros | fajadospadres.com) | ⌑ H7*

THE SOUTHWEST

Fishing villages by the sea, narrow terraces for growing bananas, steep vineyards, gurgling waterfalls and idyllic villages – in the island's wild west you can still experience the unspoilt natural beauty of Madeira's landscape. The mountains feature barren, high-altitude plateaus and deep-green forests: it's a paradise for hikers.

Equally exciting are the *levada* trails through the sleepy villages that lie above the coast. Old women in headscarves labour on tiny

Madalena do Mar is situated at the foot of steep banana terraces

potato fields and men climb across the terraces carrying 80kg of bananas on their shoulders. Despite the fact that both tourism and the main road are steadily encroaching towards the west, the coastline and mountains still offer plenty to discover off the beaten track. The southwest also has the most sunshine hours on the whole island, which is why you should pack your bathing costume and head for the beach!

THE SOUTHWEST

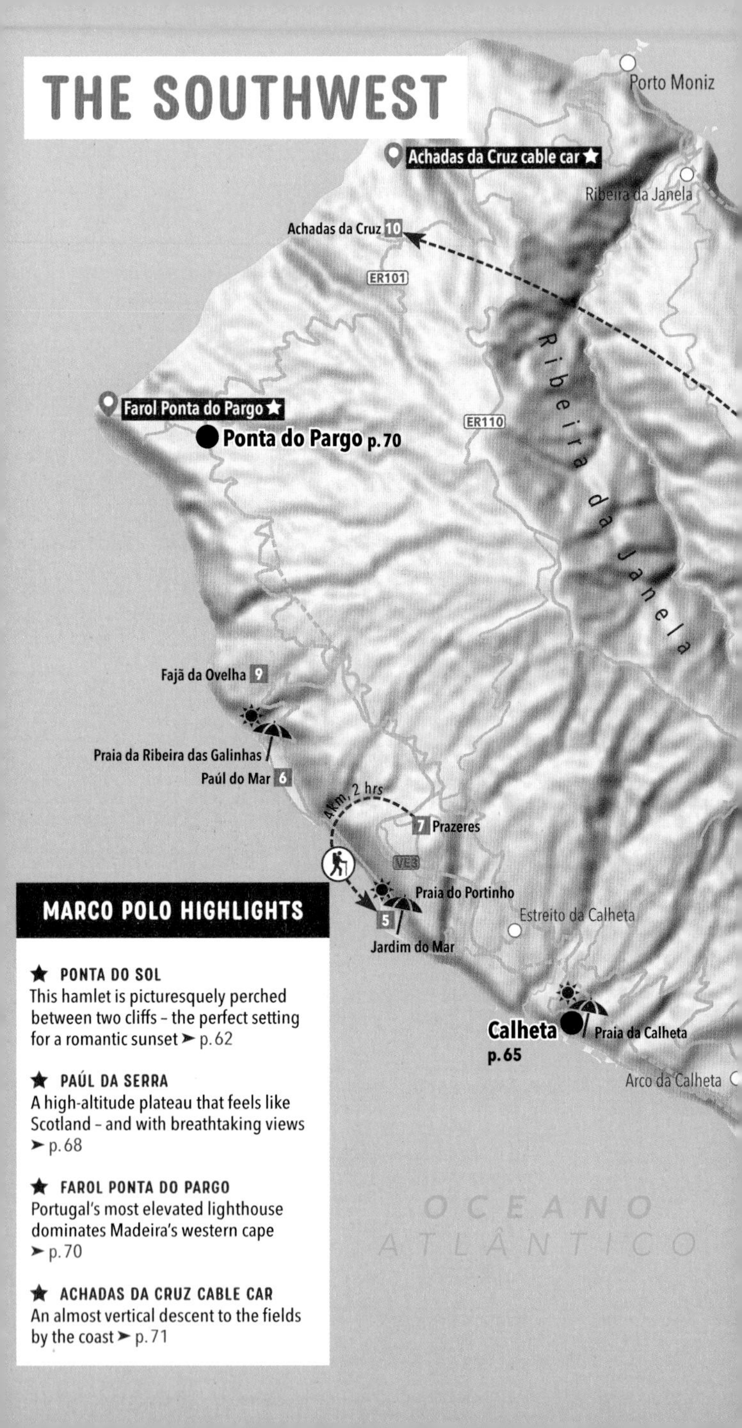

Porto Moniz

⊙ **Achadas da Cruz cable car** ★

Ribeira da Janela

Achadas da Cruz **10** ◄ - - - - - - -

ER101

R i b e i r a   d a   J a n e l a

⊙ **Farol Ponta do Pargo** ★
● **Ponta do Pargo** p. 70

ER110

Fajã da Ovelha **9**

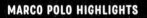
Praia da Ribeira das Galinhas
Paúl do Mar **6**

4 km, 2 hrs
7 Prazeres

VE3

🚶 Praia do Portinho
Estreito da Calheta
5
Jardim do Mar

Calheta ● Praia da Calheta
p. 65
Arco da Calheta

MARCO POLO HIGHLIGHTS

★ **PONTA DO SOL**
This hamlet is picturesquely perched between two cliffs – the perfect setting for a romantic sunset ➤ p. 62

★ **PAÚL DA SERRA**
A high-altitude plateau that feels like Scotland – and with breathtaking views ➤ p. 68

★ **FAROL PONTA DO PARGO**
Portugal's most elevated lighthouse dominates Madeira's western cape ➤ p. 70

★ **ACHADAS DA CRUZ CABLE CAR**
An almost vertical descent to the fields by the coast ➤ p. 71

O C E A N O
A T L Â N T I C O

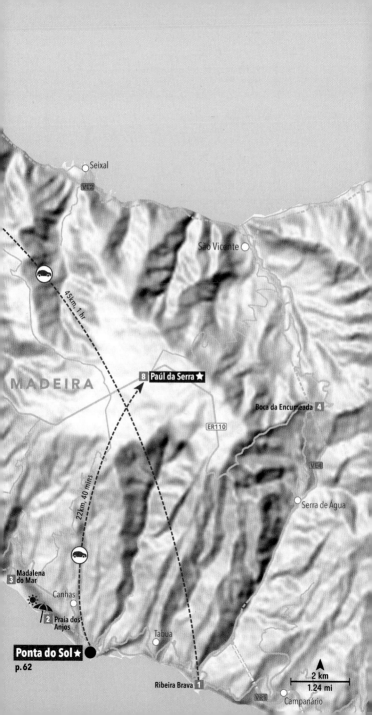

Seixal

VE2

São Vicente

45km, 1 hr

MADEIRA

8 Paúl da Serra ★

Boca da Encumeada 4

ER110

VE4

22km, 40 mins

Serra de Água

3 Madalena do Mar

Canhas

2 Praia dos Anjos

Tabua

Ponta do Sol ★
p.62

Ribeira Brava 1

2 km
1.24 mi

VR1

Campanário

PONTA DO SOL

(□ E-F7) **The "sun point" pretty much sums up ⭐ Ponta do Sol. In a place with such a name (which records the island's most sunshine hours), life has to be good.**

The old centre of the small town (pop. 4,500) perches picturesquely in a river valley between two cliffs. It comprises about two dozen houses, a cultural centre (in honour of the writer John Dos Passos whose family came from here) and, of course, the church which was consecrated to "Our Lady of the Light" in the 18th century. Slightly further uphill is a wonderful hotel – and beyond that it's terraced banana fields. You have great views of the palm-lined bay from the rocks behind the Sol Poente restaurant. To reach the rocks you need to cross an arched stone bridge. If you like romantic settings, come at sunset to enjoy the beautiful atmosphere.

EATING & DRINKING

ESTALAGEM PONTA DO SOL

This hotel and restaurant on the cliffs overlooking the coastline also welcomes non-residents. Both are minimalist and sophisticated and in a breathtaking location. If you want to treat yourself, book a table for a sunset dinner! *Quinta da Rochinha | tel. 291 970 200 | €€€*

THE OLD PHARMACY

Especially popular is the *Old Pharmacy (Rua Doutor João Augusto Teixeira 23 | mobile 927 793 866 | €)*, which is transformed from a comfortable café/bar, selling coffee, delicious cakes and hearty snacks, with a vintage souvenir shop during the day to a cool cocktail bar in the evening where the drinks are sold as "anti-depressants"!

SHOPPING

CANTINHO DE ARTES E OFICIOS

Next to the church, creative women from the village sell their handiwork – great bags, carpets and accessories. And you can watch the weavers at work. *Largo do Pelourinho | FB: Cantinho de Artes e Ofícios da Ponta do Sol*

SPORT & ACTIVITIES

LEVADA HIKE

Lombada de Ponta do Sol offers one of few *levada* hikes that can be completed as a round trip. Starting

INSIDER TIP *Refreshing round trip*

from the church next to the Solar Esmeraldo, the *Levada do Moinho* leads deep into the valley. After a steep ascent via steps, a spectacular *waterfall* awaits at the Levada Nova. The narrow track is often exposed: make sure that you have the right gear, aren't frightened of heights and are surefooted!

BEACHES

In summer, straw parasols are set up between flattened pebbles in the picturesque bay of Ponta do Sol to create a bathing beach. That's it! A beach bar caters for bathers, and there are also changing rooms and loos.

AROUND PONTA DO SOL

1 RIBEIRA BRAVA

4.7km / 8 mins by car via the VE3 main road

The "wild river" *(ribeira brava)* has created a dramatic valley where in some places there is not a lot of space between the now-tamed river and the connecting road to the north coast.

The inhabitants of the valley regularly lost their homes and property when the river swelled to a roaring torrent. But on the other hand, the village of Ribeira Brava (pop. 6,600) owes its very existence to its location at the intersection of the trading routes between the north coast and Funchal. The attractive village opens out on the sea with a charming coastal promenade and a mini fortress. Numerous cafés cater for tourist coach parties, many of whom look into the *Igreja de São Bento*, one of the oldest places of worship on the island with a Manueline pulpit and a 15th-century baptismal font. The most conspicuous

The church takes pride of place in Ponta do Sol

feature of the parish church is its steeple with a blue-and-white pattern in tiles and a globe (or armillary sphere), the symbol of the Portuguese explorers.

Madeira's folk museum, the *Museu Etnográfico da Madeira (closed Sun/ Mon | admission 3 euros | Rua de São*

Francisco 24) is housed in a fine 17th-century residence. Exhibitions in these stylish surroundings document traditional crafts, means of transport and methods of cultivating and harvesting crops on the island.

The *Restaurant & Grill Muralha (closed Mon | E R 220 1 | tel. 291 952 592 | €€)* serves artistic creations of fish and seafood. You also have marvellous views of the sea from its terrace and, if that's not enough, in summer the pebble beach below provides parasols made of palm leaves as well as wooden walkways, changing rooms, loos and even a few children's plunge pools. *▥ G7*

▣ PRAIA DOS ANJOS 🏖

2km / 5 mins by car via the ER101 coastal road

Between Ponta do Sol and Madalena do Mar, below the old ER101 coastal road (with a waterfall where you can get a free carwash!), you will find a wonderful natural pebble beach. And it has a special attraction: in high summer, a group of enthusiasts operate the *Zion Project* bar *(daily Aug/Sept | FB: thezionpontadosol)* selling snacks and drinks. On Fridays and Saturdays, in the evening, a DJ plays chillout music. Wooden walkways allow painfree access from the bar across the pebbles to the sea. *▥ E6*

▣ MADALENA DO MAR

4km / 9 mins by car via the ER101 coastal road

The route from Ponta do Sol to Madalena is an experience in itself, with the old coastal road leading directly along the oceanfront through historic tunnels. On top of that, your car will get another free wash under one of the waterfalls. If you are interested in a closer look at a banana plantation, the coastal hamlet (pop. 500) is the perfect place: the narrow track Vereda da Vargem leads from the shoreline road into the banana jungle. *▥ E6*

▣ BOCA DA ENCUMEADA

16.5km / 25 mins by car via the VE3, VE4 and ER228

On your way up to the Encumeada pass, it is worth taking a break in the legendary *Taberna da Poncha (€)* in Serra de Água where they serve a really good *poncha* and you can indulge in dropping the shells of the complimentary peanuts on the floor – which can be good fun. Some 1,000m above sea level, this "mouth" *(boca)* in the mountain range opens up to provide a thrilling panorama ranging across the north coast to the south. A number of demanding hikes start from the pass, for example a ridgeway to Pico Ruivo. *▥ H4*

INSIDER TIP
Relax with a poncha

CALHETA

(▥ C–D5) **Unadulterated beach life! Swim on the light sandy beach, stroll along the palm-lined coastal promenade at the marina in the largest town on the sun-kissed southern coast (pop. 3,100) and**

learn interesting facts about sugar cane.

Calheta spreads through a narrow river valley up the steep coast. A few brick chimneys and items of historical distillery equipment stand as a memorial to the importance of sugar cane in this town. Even today, there is a sugar cane festival after the (now much reduced) sugar cane harvest in the spring. If you want to know more about the subject, visit the exhibition *(free admission)* in the *Savoy Saccharum* hotel at the eastern edge of town: here, old photographs tell the story of how sugar cane was farmed, transported and milled in Calheta at a time when there were neither roads nor beaches.

SIGHTSEEING

IGREJA DO ESPÍRITO SANTO

The 15th-century parish church is one of the oldest on the island. While it is plain on the outside and has been renovated several times, it houses some real treasures inside: some say that the carved wooden ceiling in the Mudéjar style is even more beautiful than the one in Funchal's cathedral. The high altar features a tabernacle made of ebony and silver which was allegedly sent to Calheta on King Manuel's personal order. At Christmas, the church displays a beautiful nativity with life-size figurines and often with real livestock. *Tue–Sun 10am–1pm and 3–6pm*

SOCIEDADE DOS ENGENHOS DA CALHETA 🐗

Fans of *poncha* swear by the sugar cane spirit *(aguardente)* from Calheta that is used to mix the Madeiran mini-cocktail. It is produced here in one of the last of the island's working sugar cane mills. You can take a look *(free)* at the historical equipment, which operates around the clock

The beautiful pebble beach of Ribeira Brava with not a lounger in sight

Clean lines: the Mudas building is in keeping with the contemporary art on show

during harvest time (April and May) and learn about the history of the mill in the small *museum*. Then you can try the finished product either upstairs in the tasting room (1.20 euros incl. cake!) or in the cosy village bar *Adega do Engenho*. They serve it either as a pure spirit or in the form of *poncha*. *Mill Mon–Fri 8am–7pm, Sat/Sun 10am–7pm, bar daily 9am–midnight | Av. Dom Manuel I 29*

MUDAS. MUSEU DE ARTE CONTEMPORÂNEA 🕏

Photographers and lovers of architecture adore the work of Madeiran architect Paulo David who built the lava-grey cubes on the cliffs above Calheta in 2004. The spaces between the various parts of the building form spectacular frames that

INSIDER TIP
Framed sea views

channel your view of the coast and sea. Apart from the post-modern architecture, Madeira's most important cultural centre has changing exhibitions of contemporary art – the paintings, photographs and sculptures provide a superb outing on a rainy day. You can sit on the terrace of the museum's restaurant *Mudas Arte e Sabor (tel. 291 630 716 | €)* and enjoy a cup of coffee, snacks and a daily menu as well as the fabulous views. *Closed Mon | admission 4 euros | Estrada Simão Gonçalves da Câmara 37 | FB: MUDASmuseu |* ⏱ *1½ hrs*

EATING & DRINKING

NEW ERA
The highlights of the marina's restaurant include meat and fish dishes which are flambéed in front of you.

Their fruit desserts flambéed with Madeira wine are simply divine! In the morning you can enjoy coffee and pastries, for lunch they serve reasonably priced menus and in the late evening it's cocktails with music. *Av. Dom Manuel I/Loja 8 | tel. 291 098 138 | FB: NewEraCalheta | €€*

SPORT & ACTIVITIES

MADEIRA PARAGLIDING

Experienced paraglider Hartmut Peters offers tandem flights every afternoon (weather permitting) from approx. noon until sunset. *Rua da Achada de Santo Antão 212 | 75 euros/ flight (15–30 mins depending on the thermals) | mobile 964 133 907 | madeira-paragliding.com*

WHALE WATCHING 🐳

Baleia, baleia! You can watch these marine mammals without disturbing them either in the restored fishing boat *Ribeira Brava* or the speed boat *Stenella*. The German-Madeiran team from *Lobosonda* are involved in the protection of whales and provide statistics for scientific research. Departure times vary depending on the boat, season and weather conditions. *Adults from 44 euros, children from 22 euros | mobile 968 400 980 | lobosonda.com*

BEACHES

PRAIA DA CALHETA 🏖

On Madeira, Calheta is synonymous with beach life! Here, the island's first ever artificial sandy beach was created (including beach hotel, of course). Since then, holidaymakers and local people have been coming to Madeira's sun coast every summer to enjoy the golden (African) sand.

AROUND CALHETA

🔢 JARDIM DO MAR

6km / 10 mins by car via the VE3/ ER223

The fishing hamlet (pop. 200) is picturesquely scattered across the crescent-shaped coastal plateau below steep cliff faces. In order to visit the narrow lanes, you first need to park your car. If the car park by the Jardim do Mar hotel is full, you can leave your vehicle by the small harbour *(portinho)*. From there you can stroll along the modern 700-m promenade where you may spot the first surfers who are braving the professional-sized offshore waves. Steep steps and twisting lanes lead uphill to the *church* which, in its present form, was only consecrated in 1907.

We recommend that you have a break in *Joe's Bar (closed Sun | Vereda do Poço Velho | mobile 966 130 208 | €)*, a cosy pub/restaurant in the main lane. It has a jungle-like courtyard and serves delicious natural juices as well as excellent fish and meat dishes which will satisfy even the hungriest of surfers. Otherwise, try the *Portinho* restaurant *(Rua do Portinho | tel. 291 827 135 | €)* by the small harbour, which specialises in snacks and seafood and offers the best sea views in town.

If you want to bathe in Jardim do Mar, the *Praia do Portinho* is one of the best beaches on the southwest coast in summer, and the jetty allows you to get into the crystal-clear water easily. Admittedly, the concreted areas, which are fitted with parasols during the hot months, aren't pretty, but they are much easier for putting down your bath towels than the usual pebbles. *B5*

6 PAÚL DO MAR
9km / 14 mins by car via the VE3/ ER223

A huge rubber tree provides shade in the village square of Paúl do Mar (pop. 900), located at the foot of steep cliffs. The older inhabitants like to meet in the square at sunset for a chat. By the harbour, a statue and the colourful fishing boats provide a reminder that the locals were once all dependent on fishing, and some still are. The numbered lanes in the historical village centre have been upgraded with wonderful paving stones.

Delicious fish dishes are served in the rustic *Sol e Mar* restaurant *(Av. Pescadores Paulenses 80a | tel. 291 872 140 | €–€€)* with sea views. At the very end of the long (and not-so-pretty) coastal road, one of the island's coolest bars awaits: the colourful surfers' café *Maktub (closed Wed | Av. Pescadores Paulenses 160 |*

tel. 915 869 898) is THE place to have a fantastic mojito accompanied by reggae music while admiring the spectacular sunset. Every year in early May, the bar hosts the now-legendary *Maktub Soundsgood Festival* when international reggae stars travel to the small village of Paúl do Mar. If you love swimming in the deep southwest, the *Praia da Ribeira das Galinhas* with its coarse pebbles provides the last, and arguably coolest, opportunity to enter the sea. In summer, wooden walkways make accessing the ocean easier, but you can also use the jetty. Thankfully, the Maktub bar operates a stall on the beach with music and drinks. *B4*

INSIDER TIP
Reggae heaven

7 PRAZERES
8km / 12 mins by car via the VE3

The only attraction of the "scarecrow village" (pop. 700) – there seems to be one on every corner – is the animal and plant park *Quinta Pedagógica dos Prazeres (admission adults 1 euro, children up to 10 free | 1 hr)*. It is hidden behind the twin-spire *parish church* and run by the parish. The park is a great place for your children to get close to chickens, pigs, tortoises, rabbits and donkeys. The adjacent café *(€)*, which is really cosy due to a huge fireplace, sells local products such as marmalade. *C4*

8 PAÚL DA SERRA ★
9km / 25 mins by car via the ER211 to Rabaçal car park

This plateau might remind you of

moorland in the uplands of Britain. Only sturdy plants such as grasses, gorse and bracken can cope with the inhospitable climate at an altitude of almost 1,400m. The ground here stores rainwater like a sponge and is the source of *levadas* which distribute water to many parts of the island and channel it to hydroelectric plants. It is for this reason that a huge, recently built reservoir now spoils the landscape; but electricity needs to be generated somewhere … The dozens of wind turbines, their blades rotating in the sky, are sadly not quite sufficient to satisfy Madeira's demand for power. In good weather, there are stunning views into the valleys and across the plateau from the scenic road. In the island's famous laurel forest valley, around the forester's lodge of *Rabaçal* (see p. 122), you'll encounter crowds of *levada* hikers when the weather is good. *F4*

Get a feeling of freedom above the clouds on the Paúl da Serra upland plain

Full moon above the *farol*

PONTA DO PARGO

(⬚ A2–3) **The most beautiful lighthouse *(farol)* on Madeira is situated on the west coast and is the principal attraction of the community of Ponta do Pargo (pop. 900) that is scattered over six districts.**

This village on the western tip of Madeira is named after a tasty kind of bream called *pargo*, which is abundant in the local waters. The modest village centre of Ponta do Pargo lies around the *Igreja de São Pedro*. Its wooden ceiling is colourfully painted, showing donkeys in heaven (or in the sea?) and the beautiful local landscape. Directly below the church is the slightly oversized *Centro Cívico*: basically it's the mayor's office, but it also incorporates a health centre. With its modern architecture it appears somewhat out of place. This sleepy end of the island is awakened only once every year when, in September, the famous apple festival *(Festa do Pêro)* is celebrated.

SIGHTSEEING

FAROL ★

This is the most elevated lighthouse in Portugal: since 1922, the 15-m-tall building has been towering on steep cliffs with a 312-m-high drop to the sea – and what a view! A narrow track leads to the rocky outcrop from where you can see wide and far across the green mountain slopes. At the base of the lighthouse is a ☛ *permanent exhibition (daily 9.30am–noon and 2–4.30pm | admission free | ⏱ 15 mins)* featuring photos of lighthouses on the island. Every Wednesday afternoon, the lighthouse keeper guides visitors up the spiral staircase and explains the workings of the 1,000-watt beam and the Fresnel lenses.

INSIDER TIP
An enlightening lesson

EATING & DRINKING

A CARRETA ⚑

Simple, traditional country restaurants often prove to be the best when you are looking for rustic specialities that are typical of the island. Here they serve excellent *espetadas* (beef skewers). And, befitting for a village restaurant, christenings and weddings are celebrated here as well, while hikers in their muddy boots are always welcome as well. *Lombada Velha | tel. 291 882 163 | €-€€*

O FORNO

The Bennett family will cater to all their guests' culinary needs, whether you choose a juicy steak from the open wood fire or a vegetarian dish. Their apple-coconut-chili crumble is a delight. Afterwards, you must try the *poncha*, which is fantastic! *Closed Mon | Estrada Ponta do Pargo 316 | Salão | tel. 291 098 341 | FB: BBQOFORNO | €-€€*

INSIDER TIP
Exotic crumble

AROUND PONTA DO PARGO

🟥 FAJÃ DA OVELHA

7.5km / 15 mins by car via the ER101
The widely scattered village (pop. 1,100) is perched on a hilltop high above the Atlantic. The Massape quarter commands a fine view of the cliffs, with Paúl and Jardim do Mar at the bottom. For the delicious *poncha* (and for almost everything else you may need), go to the *Moinho snack bar (€)* in the Maloeira quarter. *□□ B4*

🔟 ACHADAS DA CRUZ

13km / 23 mins by car via the ER101
A modern ★ cable car *(teleférico)* is the principal attraction of the sleepy hamlet of Achadas da Cruz (pop. 160). The cabins of the cable car sway downwards, almost vertically, for five minutes to cover the difference in height (451m) to the fields by the rocky coast below *(daily 8am-noon and 2-6pm, in summer until 8pm | return journey 3 euros)*. If you prefer to walk, follow the hiking track downhill (return journey 4.5km). *(□□ B-C 1-2)*

WHERE TO STAY IN THE SOUTHWEST

CAMP BETWEEN BANANA PLANTS …

… fruit trees and a waterfall. At the tropical mini-glamping site of *Canto das Fontes* near Ponta do Sol, nature lovers sleep in luxurious tipis and relax in hammocks or by the pool. The organic plantation offers all of this with the background soundtrack of rolling waves on the pebble beach of Praia dos Anjos 100m below. It's quite an experience! *Caminho dos Anjos | cantodasfontes.pt | €€*

THE NORTH

A GREEN NATURAL PARADISE

Between Porto Moniz and Porto da Cruz, the island's rugged side becomes apparent: the coast is steeper, the ocean is wilder, a strong wind often blows and almost twice as much rain falls as in the south. This also means that the north is twice as green!

The north is fertile: people once created terraces on even the steepest slopes, and on many of them fruits, vines and vegetables are still grown today. Deep green valleys stretch right up into the mountains with their pointed rocky peaks, barren upland plateaus,

Terraced fields near Boaventura

waterfalls and jungles of laurisilva forest. For a long time people could reach the south only by sea or via paths across the mountains. This led to the emergence of strong, coherent village communities in the north with all the facilities they needed to exist. Today, tunnels connect them with Funchal, and many people commute there each day for their jobs. However, life in the villages has kept its rural character – and those who live here are not easily flustered by the tricks that the weather plays when the trade winds blow.

THE NORTH

Lava pools ★
● **Porto Moniz** p.76

ER101

1 Ribeira da Janela

Praia de Seixal / Poço das Lesmas
2 **Fanal** ★
3 Seixal

VE2

4 Chão da Ribeira

● **São Vicente** p.8[

Grutas de São Vicente ★

25km, 35 mins

ER209

MADEIRA

Ribeira da Janela

ER110

ER228

MARCO POLO HIGHLIGHTS

★ **LAVA POOLS**
Swimming among the volcanic rocks –
natural pools in Porto Moniz ➤ p.77

★ **FANAL**
Ancient gnarled laurel trees grow in the
fairy forest of Fanal ➤ p.78

★ **GRUTAS DE SÃO VICENTE**
Lava tunnels lead you into the bowels of
the island ➤ p.81

★ **CASAS DE COLMO**
Thatched and brightly coloured
dwellings are the main attraction in
Santana ➤ p.83

★ **PICO RUIVO**
Madeira's highest summit is accessible
to walkers ➤ p.84

Serra de Água

VE

Tabua

Campanário

Ribeira Brava

Quinta Grande

OCEANO ATLÂNTICO

5 Ponta Delgada **9** Arco de São Jorge
Boaventura
ER101
8 São Jorge
Ilha
VE1

● **Santana** p.82
Casas de Colmo ★

Queimadas **6**
15km, 30 mins
10 Faial

Praia da Alagoa
11 Porto da Cruz

São Roque do Faial

7 ● **Pico Ruivo** ★

55km, 1½ hrs
ER103

Santo António da Serra

○ Curral das Freiras

○ Jardim da Serra
○ Camacha

○ Estreito de Câmara de Lobos

VR1
○ Caniço

○ Câmara de Lobos ○ **Funchal**

↑
2 km
1.24 mi

The lava pools are great for relaxing by the wild ocean

PORTO MONIZ

(▥ D1) **When Mother Nature created Madeira, she almost forgot a
proper bathing spot! To put this
right, she made the volcano erupt
one more time: its lava flows slowly
but steadily extended out into the
sea, forming natural pools. As a
result, a plateau was created for the
island's most remote community in
the northwest, Porto Moniz (pop.
1,700), as well as Madeira's most
stunning natural pools.**

If you want to gain an overview of
the village, which was founded by the
knight Francisco Moniz in the 16th
century, drive on the mountain road,
direction west, and stop at the
Miradouro da Santa: the views here
are breathtaking! This road, as well as
the coastal road, was only built in the
1950s – before that Porto Moniz could
only be reached by boat or via
footpaths.

SIGHTSEEING

COASTAL PROMENADE

The number one attraction here are
the lava pools, although the weather is
not always suitable for bathing. But
there are many other good reasons to
visit Porto Moniz. When the sea is
rough and the surf is wild, huge waves
crashing onto the black rocks make
spectacular photographs. You get the
best view of these forces of nature
from the coastal promenade, the
Passeio Público Marítimo. If the
weather gets too bad, there are a
couple of indoor attractions: in the
🏖 🎭 *Aquário da Madeira (daily
10am–6pm | admission adults 7 euros,
children 4 euros,* 🐷 *combined ticket
with the Science Centre: adults 8 euros,
children 5 euros | Rua Forte São João*

Batista 7A | ⏱ 1 hr) in the old Forte São João Batista next to the harbour, you can marvel at the sharp teeth of the Tiger Moray Eel and watch the cleaner shrimp pick parasites off other fish. The 🎦 *Centro de Ciência Viva (daily 10am–6pm | admission adults 3.50 euros, children 2.50 euros, 🐗 combined ticket with the Science Centre: adults 8 euros, children 5 euros | Rotunda do Ilhéu Mole | ⏱ 30 mins),* or Science Centre, houses an exhibition about the laurel forests that is mainly directed towards groups of school children.

EATING & DRINKING

Numerous restaurants along the coastal promenade offer traditional Madeiran cooking, particularly fish and *lapas grelhadas* (limpets).

CACHALOTE

This restaurant on a lava promontory next to the small natural pools is in prime location. The adjacent 🎦 *mini-museum* tells you the story of sperm whale *(cachalotes)* hunting in past centuries. *Rua do Forte de São João Batista | tel. 291 853 180 | restaurantecachalote.com | €€*

SEA VIEW

Many restaurants offer seating directly above the beach, such as the popular restaurant in the *Hotel Aqua Natura | Rotunda da Piscina 3 | tel. 291 640 100 | €€).*

INSIDER TIP
Eye to eye with the surf

SNACK-BAR RESTAURANTE SALGUEIRO

The cuisine here is slightly more rustic than in other restaurants in Porto Moniz, and this is reflected in the bigger helpings – and lower prices. They also have a selection of savoury and sweet snacks. There are sea views from the first floor above the tourist information centre. *Lugar do Tenente 34 | tel. 291 850 080 | €€*

SPORT & ACTIVITIES

LEVADA HIKE

Above Porto Moniz, a wonderful *levada* hike with waterfalls and laurel forest awaits. Starting in the *Lamaceiros* quarter, the *Levada da Ribeira da Janela* leads you deep into the Ribeira da Janela valley. If you return after the second tunnel, the entire trip covers approx. 12km.

BEACHES

You can swim all year round in the ⭐ 🚩 *lava pools (Piscinas Naturais) (daily 9am–7pm; winter 9am–5pm | admission 1.50 euros)* which have numerous concrete areas for sunbathing, even in winter when the sea is slightly cooler and you have the pool almost to yourself. There are also lifeguards, onsite changing rooms and (cold) showers. Although these facilities are not available at the 🐗 pools by the *Cachalote* restaurant *(admission free),* you will probably see more fish here (splashed over the wall at high tide) if you have a face mask and snorkel.

AROUND PORTO MONIZ

1 RIBEIRA DA JANELA

3km / 6 mins by car via the VE2

At the mouth of a stream that joins the sea east of Porto Moniz, a finger-shaped rock points to the sky. It has a small window-like opening *(janela),* which has given the stream its name.

INSIDER TIP
Photo at the "window" rock

This spot is great for taking photographs of waves crashing onto the rocks. On the other side of the stream, a hydro power station uses water from the Levada da Ribeira da Janela to generate electricity. It is hard to believe that this stream (and its many tributaries) over time has created this huge green valley, which stretches up to Rabaçal and is covered in thick lush laurel forest.

If you want to get an overview of this wild landscape, drive uphill on the ER209 to the scattered hamlet of *Ribeira da Janela* (pop. 230) which nestles on the mountain slope. The many steep terraces, some of which are covered in broom heather to protect them from the salty sea air, indicate that people here still live from agriculture and winegrowing. The *Miradouro da Eira da Achada* offers spectacular views of the north coast. ≿ *D1*

2 FANAL ★

14km / 23 mins by car via the ER209 to the forestry station

If you continue to drive uphill from Ribeira da Janela, you get to Fanal, one of the most unspoilt and greenest areas on the island. Not far from the forestry station you will find fabulous ancient laurel trees – and when it is a little foggy, the entire slope changes into a magical fairy wood. Several hiking trails converge at the forestry station, for example the deep green *Levada dos Cedros*, which leads downhill towards Ribeira da Janela, or the *Vereda do Fanal* that winds itself to

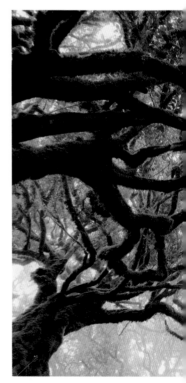

the upland plateau of Paúl da Serra, offering more wonderful views. *D–E3*

3 SEIXAL
8.5km / 11 mins by car via the VE2

It is easy to pass Seixal (pop. 650) unnoticed because the tunnelled main road keeps any through traffic out of this pretty village of vineyards situated on a lava plateau at the foot of a steep green cliff. However, bypassing Seixal would be a shame because, due to its wild coastline of lava promontories, it is a real gem, especially if you like bathing.

The black sandy beach of ★ *Praia de Seixal* next to the pier doesn't see crowds of tourists because the narrow lane down to the *Clube Naval* with its relaxing rock pool and to the sandy beach (yes, real sand!) is impassable for tourist coaches. You can also bathe on the protected *Praia das Lajes* (accessible from the western edge of the village via the Rua do Porto da Laje) or in the wonderful natural rock pool ★ *Poço das Lesmas* below the post office. Freshly caught fish is served in the *Solmar* restaurant *(Sítio da Ponte | tel. 291 854 854 | residenciasolmar. com.pt | €–€€). E2*

In the fog, the laurisilva becomes an enchanted place

A well-lit journey into the interior of the volcano: the Grutas de São Vicente

❹ CHÃO DA RIBEIRA
12km / 15 mins by car via the VE2 / mountain road

From Seixal, a few minutes a steep and winding road leads you uphill into the fertile dead-end valley. Suddenly, you enter a different world: small barns, countless fields and terraces and a few farmhouses – up here, people are still working the land. In addition, a surprising number of townspeople come here at the weekend to passionately tend their inherited plots of land. Take a break in the rustic village pub *Casa de Pasto Justiniano (tel. 291 854 559 | casade pastojustiniano.com | €–€€)* and let yourself be spoiled with fresh trout and delicious meat skewers. *⚏ E2–3*

INSIDER TIP
Rustic & delicious

SÃO VICENTE

(⚏ G–H3) **The tiny centre of the pretty small town of São Vicente (pop. 3,400) is so well concealed behind a cliff that you have to look hard not to miss it.**

While the coastal promenade and walkway through the greenery alongside the river are generously wide, the neat little houses in the old town are squeezed into a few narrow alleyways surrounding the parish church.

SIGHTSEEING

CAPELINHA DO CALHAU
In 1692 a striking little chapel dedicated to St Vincent was built into the rock that stands where the Ribeira de São Vicente flows into the sea. Mosaics

made with pebbles from the beach adorn the Baroque façade.

IGREJA DE SÃO VICENTE

Even the artistic cobblestones in front of the church entrance are dedicated to St Vincent. One section shows the body of the martyr, accompanied only by two ravens, in a boat that, according to legend, was washed ashore in southern Portugal. The sanctuary and side altars of this 18th-century church are decorated with the gilded carvings *(talha dourada)* typical of Portuguese Baroque. A beautiful *azulejo* frieze adorns the walls, and the painting on the ceiling of the nave shows St Vincent blessing the village that bears his name.

GRUTAS DE SÃO VICENTE
★ ♼ ♨

How about a trip to the interior of the island? You will travel into the geological past of Madeira on a guided tour (Portuguese/English) through the 700-m-long lava tunnel system. The easily accessible Grutas de São Vicente are caves that were created during a volcanic eruption 890,000 years ago and they offer a number of striking features. In the adjoining *Centro do Vulcanismo (daily 10am–7pm | admission adults 8 euros, children (5–14) 6 euros | Sítio do Pé do Passo | grutas ecentrodovulcanismosaovicente.com | ☺ 2 hrs)*, you can learn more about volcanic phenomena in general and the origins of the island – as well as travelling into the interior of the earth in a lift!

CAPELINHA NOSSA SENHORA DA FÁTIMA

This church is different from all the others, because it consists of only a belfry which rises into the sky on a hill. It was built by members of the local congregation in the 1950s in honour of Our Lady of Fátima. In this way, the faithful had their own Fátima chapel, which meant that there was no longer a need to make a pilgrimage to the mainland. Climb up the steps to the belfry and enjoy the fabulous views of the valley.

INSIDER TIP
Amazing 360-degree views

EATING & DRINKING

LAVRADOR SÃO VICENTE

This recent discovery is a bit off the beaten track, but the sensational views of the valley through the restaurant's panoramic glass panes and the creative and ambitious cuisine are ample reward for the winding ascent! You would not expect such refined variations of the island's classics in this rustic landscape. Gourmet cuisine at village pub prices! *Rua Eng. Perry Vidal 149 | Ginjas | tel. 291 631 163 | FB: ChefMauricioNeves | €€*

QUEBRA MAR

While you eat your hearty fish soup, the waves are breaking right next to you on the pebble beach… This inn really has the best location in the village and the finest view of the north coast. *Sítio do Calhau | tel. 291 842 338 | restaurantequebramar.com | €-€€*

AROUND SÃO VICENTE

🖪 PONTA DELGADA

7.5km / 11 mins by car via the VE1/ ER101

Once a year, the otherwise tranquil village (pop. 1,400) experiences a mass invasion: on the first Sunday in September, pilgrims and islanders keen on festivities arrive to venerate the wooden figure of *Senhor Bom Jesus* or to simply to enjoy one of the largest church festivals on the island.

The crucifix is said to have been washed up here in the 15th century in a chest. The church that was erected on the spot where it was found burned down almost completely in 1908, and the flames spread to the crucifix too. Its charred remains were saved and are kept in a glass case in the new *church*, which is decorated in the Baroque style.

The area surrounding Ponta Delgada is well suited for hiking away from the crowds, for example on the old connecting track of the Caminho Real towards São Jorge. Otherwise, you can hike through the laurel jungle: in the neighbouring village of *Boaventura*, a wonderful levada leads into the green valley, and if you like, you can cross the main ridge in the direction of Curral das Freiras. *⑭ J2*

Living history: *casas de colmo* in Santana

SANTANA

(⑭ L–M 2–3) **Santana, the small town (pop. 3,500) with the photogenic thatched, wooden houses, features on every postcard and is a must-see for guided coach tours. So you can expect crowds of tourists by the showpiece houses in the village centre. However, Santana has more to offer.**

It owes its name to Saint Anne, and the church is also dedicated to her. In Santana it is easy to forget that this is actually the district centre because it has a true village feel. In fact, with the exception of the tourist coaches by the town hall, Santana is still a rural place.

SIGHTSEEING

CASAS DE COLMO ★

Until a few decades ago, many of the *casas de colmo*, with their distinctive triangular shape and thatched roofs, were inhabited by whole families who led a spartan life characterised by working outdoors. The micro-dwellings were practical for labourers who were hired by landowners to work the fields on the fertile north coast. After the harvest had been brought in, these farmworkers would take their houses down and move on. Some of the houses were kept and used as sheds. Today, only those houses which have been extended in recent times are still lived in. One of the 👉 showpiece dwellings next to the town hall displays some original furniture, while another one is an arts and crafts shop. You can find a picturesque but quirky setting for garden gnomes in the home of Senhor Manuel *(Rua Dr João Abel de Freitas Médico)*, which you may visit while enjoying his home-made liqueur.

INSIDER TIP
Coffee liqueur in a 'quirky' house

PARQUE TEMÁTICO DA MADEIRA 👪

How about a go on a trampoline or a pedal boat, or a bouncy flight across the island in a simulator? Not far from the village centre, this popular theme park has informative attractions mainly aimed at families. The pavilions feature aspects of the culture and history of Madeira, and hungry explorers are also catered for. *Daily 10am–6pm, in summer until 7pm | admission adults 6 euros, children 4 euros | Fonte da Pedra | parque tematicodamadeira.pt | ⏱ 3 hrs*

ROCHA DO NAVIO

At the foot of the plateau of Santana is a nature reserve, flanked by waterfalls, where you will meet very few people. Down here, between small fields and farmhouses, it is just idyllic and is a great place for a picnic. There is a cable car *(daily 9am–1pm and 2–6pm, in summer and at weekends until 7pm | return ticket 5 euros)* that runs from the rocks down to the coarse pebble beach. Or you can also hike downhill (be careful: the track is steep and can be slippery) and then return by cable car (3 euros).

INSIDER TIP
Make time for a picnic

EATING & DRINKING

CANTINHO DA SERRA

This rustic country inn offers a cosy interior which is particularly welcoming in winter when the open fire is crackling. The servings of hearty dishes such as octopus with onions and braised kid in a clay pot are substantial and often enough for two. *Estrada do Pico das Pedras | tel. 291 573 727 | €€*

QUINTA DO FURÃO

Enjoy the stillness of nature! This friendly hotel is situated in remote tranquillity on the edge of a steep cliff, surrounded only by vineyards and vegetable fields. There are magnificent views along the north coast, especially from the coastal hiking trail that runs past the hotel. The restaurant offers top-class cuisine using locally grown (and partly their own) produce. *Estrada Quinta do Furão 6 | tel. 291 570 100 | quinta dofurao.com | €€*

SERRA E MAR 🚩

This traditional family restaurant serves marine delicacies such as black scabbard fish as well as mountain cuisine. The prices are reasonable and the servings generous – no wonder it enjoys such popularity with the local villagers. *Rua Baixo da Igreja | tel. 291 573 895 | €*

SPORT & ACTIVITIES

The north of the island has countless hiking trails, and a single holiday on Madeira will not be enough to explore them all. The ancient connecting trails of the *Caminho Real*, which lead from one village to the next along the coast, are particularly beautiful.

If you would like to hike along the coast, start at the Quinta do Furão and walk along the spectacular steep cliff coast in a westerly direction. With numerous bends, the Caminho Real snakes its way downhill to the *Calhau de São Jorge*.

AROUND SANTANA

6 QUEIMADAS

6km / 12 mins by car to the Rancho Madeirense via the Caminho das Queimadas

From the car park of the *Rancho Madeirense* holiday village (on the road to Pico das Pedras), a shady path leads about 2km along a *levada* and through green laurel woodland to the *Queimadas Forest Lodge*. From Santana, a narrow lane leads up to a former charcoal-burners' settlement (chargeable car park). This is a picturesque spot with ponds and picnic tables, located at an altitude of 900m in a clearing surrounded by rhododendrons. It is the starting point of the wonderful laurel forest hike along the *Levada do Caldeirão Verde* (four-hour return trip). Sure-footed hikers with a head for heights can continue hiking from the "Green Cauldron" to the *Caldeirão do Inferno*, the "Cauldron of Hell" (an additional two hours there and back). �🕮 *L3*

7 PICO RUIVO ⭐

10km / approx. 20 mins by car to the trail car park of Achada do Teixeira

Madeira's highest mountain (1,862m) is the last stop on a wonderful hike via Achada do Teixeira. If the weather is kind, the panorama from the summit is breathtaking. The ascent to the peak on a paved path is not difficult and takes no more than one hour. The refuge just below the

Quinta do Furão: with such marvellous views you might forget to eat

summit sells snacks (daily, except in bad weather).

Walkers who are fit and have the right equipment can press on to the 1,818-m tall *Pico do Arieiro* (⌖ *K5*). In early summer a unique display of endemic alpine flowers – including yellow Madeira violets – can be seen here, whereas in winter it can snow at times. On your return, you can stop in the *Abrigo da Heidi (Achada do Teixeira | FB: Abrigo da Heidi | €€)* at the trail car park of Achada do Teixeira where the Austrian landlords serve not just Madeiran classics but also Alpine specialities. ⌖ *K4*

ⓑ SÃO JORGE

7km / 12 mins by car via the ER101
The main attraction of the village (pop. 1,500) is the *Igreja de São Jorge*. With its gilded Baroque carvings and 18th-century tiled frieze, this parish church is regarded as the most beautiful and artistically valuable place of worship in the north of the island. The fact that a bishop of Funchal once had his summer retreat here may have helped! Directly behind the church, a typical, rectangular thatched house harbours a little restaurant, the *Casa de Palha (Achada Grande | tel. 291 576 382 | €)*, where diners are served skilfully prepared regional dishes. Be sure to try the *consomé de camarão no pão*, a creamy shrimp soup in a bread bowl.

From the church, a road leads to the *Ponta de São Jorge*, jutting into the sea with its lighthouse *(farol)*. From the former whale hunting lookout of Ponta Vigia near the lighthouse,

A view for eagles and pirates: Penha de Águia

you can enjoy undisturbed coastal views.

If you want to have a closer look at the sea, walk down to the coastal path, and from the *Cabo Aereo Café (Parque de Merendas Farrobo | tel. 291 575 209 | €)* the ancient *Caminho Real* connecting track that zig-zags its was downhill. In theory, you should be able to take a beautiful coastal round trip with a detour to the old jetty at the Ponta de São Jorge. However, if that is too much, you can just take the road down to the sea. At the Ribeira de São Jorge, a sign points to the *Piscina* and the *Ruinas*. The latter are the photogenic remains of the old *sugar cane mill*, and next door a public swimming pool is awaiting its re-opening. If the sea is calm, bathing is also lovely in the small lagoon where the Ribeira joins the ocean. *L2*

9 ARCO DE SÃO JORGE
16km / 25 mins by car via the ER101
The small village (pop. 420) stretches like a painted arch across a high-altitude valley, framed by the sea and mountains.

The lookout point *Cabanas* on the road to Arco de São Jorge affords a dizzying vantage point. Farmers often sell tropical fruit here to tourists who come to take photos. Shortly before Arco de São Jorge, flower lovers should visit the *rose garden (Roseiral)* of the *Quinta do Arco (April–Nov daily 11am–6pm | admission 5 euros | Sítio da Lagoa)* with over 1,700 different species. *K2*

10 FAIAL
6km / 15 mins by car via the old mountain road
If you don't take the tunnelled route to

Faial, but follow the old mountain road instead, you will have countless scenic views. Amidst terraces of grapevines and orchards, this charming village (pop. 1,600) nestles at the foot of a mountain by the sea – the 600-m *Penha de Águia* (Eagle Rock).

INSIDER TIP
Commanding views

From the small *Fortim, a miradouro* with a few old cannons, you get a great view of the mountain.

If the prospect of trout in bacon in a cosy wicker-chair atmosphere sounds enticing, stop at the *Casa de Chá do Faial (Lombo do Baixo | tel. 291 572 223 | FB: Restaurante Casa de Chá do Faial | €€)*. The locals as well as tour operators appreciate this restaurant in the upper quarter of São Roque do Faial with its furnishings of wood and basketwork and a great view from the roof terrace. Teenagers will appreciate the 🎯 *Kartódromo do Faial (daily 10am–6pm, in summer until 7pm | cart hire 18 euro/15 mins, from age 14 | Estrada da Praia do Faial | akmadeira.com)* is near the mouth of the Ribeira do Faial and is run by a club who always welcome guests.

For bathing, simply pass the cart track and you are on the "beach". The man-made bathing cove next to the mouth of the river is perfectly protected from the rough seas of the north. In summer, you can put your towels down on the concreted sunbathing areas and access the water via the ramp. A café sells snacks and drinks. *M–N3*

11 PORTO DA CRUZ

9.5km / 12 mins by car via the VE2

The port *(porto)* of the cross *(cruz)* that was erected by the first inhabitants is one of the oldest settlements on the island, today with a population of 2,600. There is a wonderful walking route along the small promenade, beginning at the esplanade cafés at the eastern pebble beach and leading to the swimming area popular in summer and the tiny "harbour". Porto da Cruz offers the best bathing on Madeira's north coast, and the *seawater swimming pool (only open in summer | admission approx. 2 euros)* on the promenade is particularly lovely. If you want to swim in the sea, access is good in the most westerly cove of the pebbly 🌴 *Praia da Alagoa* where you find some black sand mixed in underneath the surf-polished stones. The scenery is breathtaking because you swim exactly beneath the steep 500-m cliff of Eagle's Rock. Thanks to generally suitable conditions for surfing beginners, Porto da Cruz has become the second-best surfing hotspot on the island (see "Sport and activities").

At the Praia da Alagoa you will immediately see the 🐑 *sugar mill*, which is one of the few remaining mills on the island and can be visited free of charge. You are welcome to taste the high-proof finished products in the adjoining shop. A good place to stop off is the rustic inn *A Pipa (Casas Próximas | mobile 968 527 400 | €–€€)*. Landlord Zé is well known among Madeirans for his particularly tasty fish dishes. *N4*

THE EAST

RICH IN CONTRAST

The eastern part of Madeira displays an incredible diversity of landscapes, with a new valley and a fresh view over the next bay every few kilometres.

Cool green hills are contrasted with barren desert-coloured earth, and contemporary architecture is paired with traditional crafts. The gentle bays of the east were the first landing sites for explorers and pirates: the places between Caniço and the Ponta de São Lourenço are more steeped in history than other parts of the island.

The easternmost tip of the island: Ponta de São Lourenço

You are also highly likely to begin your journey in the east since this is where the airport is located. The future of the island is most visible in this region: the container port at the former whaling station of Caniçal, the exclusive marina settlement of Quinta do Lorde, and the industrial areas bordering the highway leading to the west of the island. Unfortunately "progress" is not always attractive, but to escape the built-up coastal area you only need drive a few kilometres into the hills to find the well-preserved original Madeira.

THE EAST

São Roque do Faial
○ Porto da Cruz

MADEIRA

8 Portela

Ribeiro Frio **3** 🚗 25km, 42 mins — ER102

Santo da Serra **9**

ER202

2 Passo do Poiso

🚗

16km, 23 mins

🚗 10km, 11 mins

🚗 24km, 24 mins

ER102

🚗

Santa Cruz
p. 94

● **Camacha**
p. 92

Gaula

VR1

○ **Funchal**

Praia dos Reis Magos

1 Caniço

MARCO POLO HIGHLIGHTS

★ **MUSEU DA BALEIA**
The whaling museum in Caniçal tells the story of these marine mammals around Madeira ➤ p. 99

★ **PONTA DE SÃO LOURENÇO**
The eastern tip of Madeira is a wonderful rocky treat for hikers ➤ p. 100

Ilhéu do Guincho

7 Ponta de São Lourenço ★

5

6 Quinta do Lorde

4 Caniçal   Prainha

📍 **Museu da Baleia** ★

Ilhéu da Cevada ou
dos Desembarcadouros

Ilhéu do Farol

Praia de Machico
● **Machico p.96**

Água de Pena
VR1

O C E A N O
A T L Â N T I C O

2 km
1.24 mi

Basket-weaving in Camacha

CAMACHA

(*N7*) **Camacha nurtures its traditions. The craft of basketry is still very much alive in the highest-lying district of Madeira. And where would the football-crazy Portugal be now if a certain son of this village had not introduced this ball sport here?**

The year 1875 is proudly commemorated at a memorial in the main square. One of the sons of the Hinton family of wine merchants had learnt to play football while studying in England and had subsequently wanted to introduce his friends in Camacha to the game. This was how the Madeirans became the first to learn to play football, a game the Portuguese could not do without today.

The small town with its population of 7,500 is situated on a fertile mountain ridge almost 700m above the sea. Apple trees are cultivated in the surrounding terraced fields, which the festival-loving inhabitants have to thank for their annual apple festival – and the sparkling *cidra* (cider). There is plenty of folklore in this area: the local dance and music groups are said to be some of the most lively on the island. It could be that 'dancing to get warm' helps to overcome the frequently damp coolness at this altitude.

SIGHTSEEING

CAFÉ RELÓGIO

While on the subject of dampness: some families still owe their livelihood to the craft of basketry: the *vimeiros* mostly sit down to work in damp cold cellars because the wicker stems are more flexible in these conditions. You can marvel at the products at the basketry market Café Relógio: some are practical (wonderful wicker furniture) and some entirely decorative (delicately made dust catchers in the form of frogs). The shop has sprung up around a now almost invisible clock tower of a former British summer residence, which explains its name ("Café Clock"). Although many products are somewhat kitsch, you will still find attractive and practical souvenirs. In the demonstration workshop in the basement you can see the skilled basket-makers at work. *Daily 9am–6pm | Largo Conselheiro Aires de Ornelas 12 | caferelogio.com*

INSIDER TIP
A basket-lover's paradise

IGREJA DA CAMACHA

After visiting the Café Relógio, it is well worth taking a look round the 'modern' Camacha nearby. When the village church on the main square became too small, the parish was provided with a new church in 1997. Its exceptional architecture is reminiscent of the Casino in Funchal, designed by Oscar Niemeyer – the inhabitants of Camacha are therefore extremely proud of their unorthodox place of worship. *Daily 9am–5pm | Sítio da Igreja*

EATING & DRINKING

RESTAURANTE O CESTO

"The Basket" is a typical old-school family inn: with a bar and café at the front and the dining area at the back. This is where you are most likely to meet the people of the village enjoying rustic Madeiran food, such as a warming wheat soup. The owner speaks good English and will help you to choose from the menu. The soup is definitely to be recommended! *Rua Maria Ascenção 95 | tel. 291 922 068 | €*

AROUND CAMACHA

🔟 CANIÇO

7km / 10 mins by car via the VE5
Caniço de Baixo with its hotel complexes, restaurants, cliff-bathing areas and promenade leading to the pebble beach of ⚓ Praia dos Reis Magos has become a popular holiday resort. The actual town centre of Caniço is 200m above sea level. Over the past three decades it has developed from a village cultivating onions (now only commemorated by the annual onion festival in May) to a town with a population exceeding 23,000. There are only a couple of original features, such as the modest parish church dating from the 18th century and a few surrounding houses.

The hotel *Quinta Splendida (Estrada da Ponta da Oliveira 11 | tel. 291 930 400 | quintasplendida.com)* is set in lush 🌳 botanical gardens below the church. Even if you are not staying at the hotel, you can still visit the fantastic garden with its attractive viewpoint and trees, flowers and herbs labelled with their botanical names. A guided tour in English is also offered once a week *(Thu 5–6pm | 5.90 euros | book at the hotel reception).*

The 5 Element Spa of the newly designed 🏊 *Galoresort (tel. 291 930 948 | galoresort.com/spa)* offers an incredible range of treatments – rather unusual for the Portuguese – including panoramic saunas (Bio and Finnish) and fantastic resting spaces with deeply relaxing sea views.

INSIDER TIP
Zen relaxation

Don't forget to go and see the *Cristo Rei do Garajau*! This statue of Christ has been standing guard above the pebble beach of *Garajau* since 1927, making it older than its big brother in Rio de Janeiro! You can also enjoy the fantastic view of Funchal. 🗺 *N8*

② PASSO DO POISO
9km / 18 mins by car via the ER203
from all four points of the compass meet at the top of the pass at an altitude of 1,400m. From here you can drive up to the Pico do Arieiro, across to Santo da Serra, down to Funchal and also to Faial. What was once a shepherd's shelter at the crossroads has recently been turned into the popular rustic restaurant *Casa de Abrigo do Poiso (tel. 291 782 269 | €)*, where the spicy bread soup *açorda* and juicy beef skewers are served in front of a roaring open fire. 🗺 *M6*

③ RIBEIRO FRIO
14km / 25 mins by car via the ER203/ ER103
On the "cold stream", a few hairpin bends to the north of the Poiso Pass, the state forestry agency has set up a trout farm and created a small botanical garden with camellias and laurel shrubs around the fishponds, which are filled with water from the stream *(admission/parking 1 euro).* Thanks to an ingenious system of sluices along the slope, the fish move from one pond to another as they increase in size until, finally, you can admire the enormous trout in a large round pool. Not far away, both fresh and smoked trout are served at the Ribeiro Frio restaurant *(9am–7pm | tel. 291 575 898 | €–€€).*

Behind the restaurant is the access to the 🚶 *Levada do Furado*, which sure-footed walkers can follow for some 11km, with wonderful views of the north coast all the way, as far as the Portela Pass. If you prefer to take a short walk, look out on the road for a yellow sign marked "Balcões". From here it takes about 30 minutes to reach a lookout point with magnificent views towards high mountains and also towards the sea. 🗺 *M5*

SANTA CRUZ

(🗺 O–P 6–7) **Most tourists only see this small but pretty coastal town (pop. 7,200) from the air for a few seconds before landing at the neighbouring airport. Despite air-**

Idyllic Santa Cruz with its fishing boats and date palms

craft noise, it is well worth making a detour to visit the pleasant Santa Cruz.

You can stroll through the attractively paved streets to the atmospheric church square with the *Igreja de São Salvador*, built in 1533, which still shows evidence of stonemasonry dating from the Manueline period. A promenade runs parallel to the sea and the shingle beach. While exploring, do not forget to pay a visit to the small *market hall*. At first sight, the building appears unpromising, but it makes for fascinating people-watching and, what's more, you can admire the agricultural and fishing scenes made of *azulejo* tiles by the Portuguese artist Outeiro Águeda.

EATING & DRINKING

TABERNA DO PETISCO

A rustic pub atmosphere, low prices, good *poncha* and delicious tapas – what more could you want? Oh yes, you might also need to book a table … because word has spread on the island about how good this tavern is! *Closed Mon | Rua Cónego César de Oliveira 23 | tel. 291 643 525 | €*

BEACHES

The *Praia das Palmeiras (admission free)* begins behind the market hall. This area is popular in summer as it has a 👶 children's plunge pool as well as access to the sea via steps. A real attraction – especially for children – is the 🐾 *Aquaparque* *(June–Sept 9am–6pm, in high summer until 7pm, admission adults 8 euros, children 5 euros | Ribeira da Boaventura | FB: Aquaparquemadeira | ⏱ 3 hrs)*, with pools, slides and artificial water courses as well as birds and reptiles. This is a great place for relaxing and having fun.

In *Ribeira da Boaventura a swimming complex* has been built with convenient access to the sea via a sheltered bay between the area for water sports and the two swimming pools.

MACHICO

(📖 P5–6) **Attractive squares and alleyways, a short but pretty coastal promenade and the light-coloured sandy beach that is Machico's pride and joy all provide an invitation to stroll around, relax and go for a swim. Madeira's oldest settlement has developed into an exciting small town (pop. 11,300) with a lively restaurant scene.**

The town is spread along the wide and fertile valley and up the steep mountain slopes. To get the best impression of the town, you should stroll along the Levada do Caniçal and take a look down the narrowest alleys: a new view across the Machico valley appears around every new corner.

In 1419, the discoverers of the island first went ashore in this bay. However, they were probably not the very first to reach the island as, according to legend, English lovers Anne Dorset and Robert Machyn had previously been stranded here. It appears that the name of the settlement Machico was taken from his surname, because the Portuguese explorers found a weather-beaten wooden cross engraved with this name. What would have been Madeira's fate if Anne had

Men playing dominos in Machico

not died soon after the couple had been unintentionally stranded and had instead given birth to a few (English) children …

SIGHTSEEING

IGREJA NOSSA SENHORA DA CONCEIÇÃO

The main parish church dates back to the 15th century. King Manuel I donated the side doorway with its three marble columns. The detailing on the main portal still reflects the Manueline period with grotesque faces symbolising good and evil. As the interior of the church was thoroughly remodelled during the Baroque era, only the two side chapels hint at its original appearance. One of the chapels displays the coat of arms of the Teixeira family. A statue of Tristão Vaz Teixeira, who ruled the eastern part of Madeira from Machico, stands on the square in front of the church.

CAPELA DOS MILAGRES

Largo dos Milagres, a square shaded by tall weeping fig trees, is the place where the first church on Madeira was built back in the year 1420. The "chapel of miracles" that stands there today dates from 1810. The previous building fell victim to disastrous floods, with the exception of the coat of arms on its gable and a doorway with a pointed arch. Fishermen miraculously salvaged the statue of Christ, which had been swept out to sea by the floods. A painting to the left of the altar depicts this event, which has been celebrated with a lively festival every October since the 1903 flood.

FORTS

In the 18th century the people of Machico tried to protect their easily accessible bay from pirate raids by constructing three forts. Two of these forts have survived: the *Forte de São João Baptista* to the east, which is not open to the public, and the triangular *Forte de Nossa Senhora do Amparo* where you can see the moat and a few canons. It is just a stone's throw from the latter to the newly developed promenade, between the new complex of the multipurpose *Forum Machico* cultural centre and the mouth of the Machico river.

PICO DO FACHO

To the east, the bay of Machico is flanked by the pointed "torch mountain", which has had its name since the days of pirate raids, when sentries would light fires on the summit to warn the population. You get to the mountain via a minor road that starts at the Caniçal tunnel and leads to the 322-m-high peak. From here you have marvellous views of the bay of Machico and the airport, but also towards Caniçal and the Ponta de São Lourenço. At weekends, the mountain is popular with local people who come here to picnic. □ P5

EATING & DRINKING

BAÍA BEACH CLUB

The terrace directly on the coast, with views of the bay and marina, is the perfect place to sit, particularly with a delicious ice-cream sundae in front of you. This is the way to enjoy life! *Porto de Recreio | mobile 914 758 975 | €€*

PASTELARIA GALÃ

The inn is a pleasant combination of bar, confectioner's shop (with fantastic pastries) and restaurant. Because of the reasonable prices and excellent food, you will meet plenty of islanders here. *Rua General António Teixeira de Aguiar 1/3 | tel. 291 965 720 | €*

RESTAURANTE LILY'S

This fantastic restaurant situated above Machico is a gastronomic revelation! Lily will personally attend to your every wish and offers dishes including a delicious fish soup, beef in Madeira sauce and the "catch of the day". *Closed Mon | Estrada D Manuel I 170 | Caramanchão | tel. 291 964 014 | restaurantelilys.com | €€*

BEACHES

Machico's greatest pride is the light-coloured sandy beach of ⭐ *Praia de Machico*, which has been created inside a protective pier using sand imported from Africa and is tremendous fun in summer. You can swim out to the blue bathing island or paddle in the shallow warm water. It's heaven!

AROUND MACHICO

④ CANIÇAL

5.5km / 12 mins by car via the ER109
For a long time Madeira's easternmost town (pop. 4,000) was a centre for fishing, whaling and boat building. Today, the large free-trade zone and the cargo port dominate the life of this

Prainha: a dreamy beach for water lovers

rapidly growing community. For a reminder of Caniçal's past as a major whaling station visit the modern ★ 🛧 🚩 *Museu da Baleia (Tue–Sun 10.30am–6pm | admission 10 euros | Rua Garcia Moniz 1 | museudabaleia. org | ⏱ 2 hrs).* This museum has information about the impressive sperm whales that were hunted and presents the history of whaling on Madeira, which continued until the 1980s. Exhibits show the stages of the whaling process, including the manual harpooning from little rowing boats and the subsequent processing of the catch.

For a snack, stop at *Muralha's Bar (tel. 291 961 468 | €)* opposite the new swimming pool, which has bags of character and mainly serves fish. In the evening (mainly local) patrons queue for their *petiscos* (tapas) fresh from the sea. 🗺 Q5

⑤ PRAINHA 🛧

10km / 10 mins by car via the VR1

The small sandy beach of Prainha, east of Caniçal, has been popular with generations of Madeirans. It is one of the few places on the island where a natural bathing beach has formed from volcanic sand. As a result, the car park, beach bar and sand are crowded in summer. If you come in winter, don't be surprised if you find that the strong surf has swallowed the sand, leaving only the bare rocks behind. Eventually, in time for the bathing season, the sea returns the precious commodity. If the weather is unsuitable for bathing, you can climb the adjacent hill. Every year, in September, the fishermen congregate here for a pilgrimage to the small chapel on the hilltop, carrying a statue of Nossa Senhora da Piedade (Our Lady of Mercy). 🗺 Q5

⑥ QUINTA DO LORDE 🛧

11km / 12 mins by car via the VR1/ ER109

This was a controversial development *(quintadolorde.pt)* as it was unclear who had approved the plans to build an artificial settlement (including a village church) attracting wealthy foreigners to this bay that is classified as a nature reserve. The complex took a long time to complete, but it is questionable whether the real estate investors got their intended return because the luxury hotel is rarely fully booked. Sailors love to drop anchor in the modern marina which has a chic restaurant and a nice café. Also, and this is really the best about Quinta do

Lorde, it is a wonderful place for exclusive bathing, featuring a pebble beach with crystal-clear water, a pool and a lounger area. The fee is 15 euros/day and that includes a sun lounger plus parasol and towel. *Q5*

7 PONTA DE SÃO LOURENÇO ★
12km / 15 mins by car to the Baía de Abra via the VE1/ER109

The eastern tip of Madeira is barren and windy. Clearing of the forest cover began here at an early date, and later the land was used to pasture goats who devoured any green shoots. As a result, the landscape is now a scene of bare hills, which are carpeted in flowers in spring, and bizarrely shaped rocks that rise from the turquoise sea, as if piled up by the hands of children, in the colours of ochre, rust-red, grey and greenish-black.

There is a picnic spot with a wonderful view of the sea and headland at *Ponta do Rosto*. The road leading to Ponta de São Lourenço ends at a car park for walkers above *Baía de Abra*. The walk to the eastern tip of the island and back reveals new scenic vistas at every twist and turn of the track.

For the finest view of the offshore islands and the lighthouse (built in 1870), you should go to the twin peaks of the 125-m-high *Ponta do Furado*, the "pierced tip" as this hill is known thanks to holes that the sea has carved out of its rocks. The ascent is very steep, but spectacular views are the reward.

You'll find an interesting visitor centre in the *Casa do Sardinha*, home to the nature reserve's park rangers, with a snack bar and (chargeable) loo. The palm trees offer a nice shady spot for a picnic. *Q–S5*

8 PORTELA
9km / 16 mins by car via the VE1/ER108

This village, strung out along the road, marks the island's watershed. Its centre consists of a taxi rank, a bus stop and a lookout point with a rustic restaurant, the *Portela à Vista (tel. 291 963 189 | €)*. From here the view across to Penha de Águia ("eagle rock") on the north coast is stunning. To the left, just behind the flower stalls, is the start of a hiking path which leads to Maroços in approximately three hours. *N5*

9 SANTO DA SERRA
8km / 17 mins by car via the ER108

Long before Robert Trent Jones designed Madeira's first golf course at Santo da Serra (or, more precisely, at Santo António da Serra), many visitors came to the attractive, usually fresh and breezy hilly countryside in which this village (pop. 950) nestles.

Sugar magnates and other wealthy Madeirans built their summer homes here. Among them was the Blandy family, wine merchants who came to the island from England. Their estate, the ☛ *Quinta do Santo da Serra*, near the church, is now public land *(admission free)*, and the Madeirans love to

The cliffs are almost vertical at Ponta de São Lourenço

INSIDER TIP
Blandy's eye view

come to its garden for a picnic. At the rear of the garden, the *Miradouro dos Ingleses* offers a panoramic view of the east of the island. From this place the Blandys once kept an eye on the ships approaching or passing by.

Every Sunday, a farmers' market is held in Santo da Serra and Madeirans come from far and wide to shop for fruit, vegetables and all kinds of other things, including clothes and garden plants.

Snacks and meat skewers are on the menu in the rustic restaurant *A Nossa Aldeia (closed Mon | Sítio dos Casais Próximos | tel. 291 552 142 | €)*.

WHERE TO STAY IN THE EAST

FLOWER POWER!

A wonderful scent of flowers wafts through the apartments of the *Quinta Splendida*. Stroll to the pool and spa through a sensational park, which easily rivals the botanic garden. And be spoilt with fresh herbs from the garden at the hotel restaurant or the gourmet *La Perla* in the old manor house. *166 rooms | Estrada da Ponta da Oliveira 11 | Caniço | tel. 291 930 400 | quintas plendida.com | €€-€€€*

PORTO SANTO

SAND, SAND & MORE SAND!

Dourada, "the golden one", is what the locals call Porto Santo, because almost 9km of fine, golden sand line the south coast of the island.

What's more, Porto Santo is dominated by a "golden" colouring because, with the exception of a few areas of forestation, there aren't many trees on this dry, barren and rocky island. This is because, for centuries, people systematically cleared the slopes of the endemic dragon trees.

Porto Santo's beaches resemble those of the Caribbean

Today, the island's 5,500 inhabitants make the best of their land-scape, growing wine in a few places, but otherwise earning a living from beach tourism in summer. During peak season, the atmos-phere is Caribbean, including fully booked all-inclusive resorts and beach bars. Those who don't just want to lie in the sun come at other times of the year, like autumn, when the weather is good, the sea is at its warmest and prices have returned to normal levels. Also, if you do some hiking, you may well discover the island's green pockets.

PORTO SANTO

Quinta das Palmeiras **5**

Campo de Baixo

Pico de Ana Ferreira **6**

6.6km, 30 mins

ER111

7 Praia do Zimbralinho

8 Ponta da Calheta

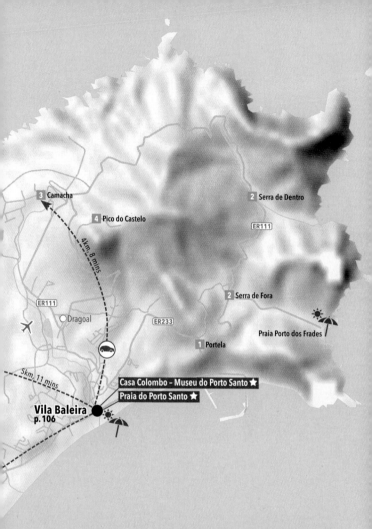

3 Camacha

4 Pico do Castelo

2 Serra de Dentro

ER111

2 Serra de Fora

4km, 8 mins

ER111

○Dragoal

ER233

Praia Porto dos Frades

1 Portela

Casa Colombo – Museu do Porto Santo ★
Praia do Porto Santo ★

5km, 11 mins

Vila Baleira
p. 106

MARCO POLO HIGHLIGHTS

★ CASA COLOMBO –
MUSEU DO PORTO SANTO
A shrine to the navigator Christopher
Columbus, who lived in this house for a
time ➤ p. 106

★ PRAIA DO PORTO SANTO
A beach of fine sand runs all the way from
the main town to Ponta da Calheta,
magically attracting summer
holidaymakers ➤ p. 108

1 km
0.62 mi

VILA BALEIRA

(□ V-W11) **Do not be surprised if the delightful main town feels more like a village. In fact, Vila Baleira (pop. 2,600) is not much bigger than a village, but it is a very attractive place to visit!**

This applies at least to the historic centre with its white houses, in whose shade suntanned old men sit to play dominoes and a colourful mix of people meet for a cup of coffee. About half of the island's residents live in this miniature metropolis by the harbour, where there are at least a few banks and supermarkets and whose pace of life is determined by the coming and going of the Madeira ferry *Lobo Marinho (portosantoline.pt)*. Everything has a sleepy feel until, in July, Vila Baleira awakes to the action when large numbers of tourists (mainly from Madeira or the Portuguese mainland) suddenly fill the atmospheric alleyways around *Largo do Pelourinho* and the palm-lined beach promenade.

SIGHTSEEING

LARGO DO PELOURINHO

INSIDER TIP
Soft and delicious

At "pillory square" you should first of all head to Lambecas to buy one of the island's best ice creams. They've been selling them here since 1958! The beautiful buildings of the old town along with the palm trees and intricately plastered compass dial make a pretty subject for a photograph. The former *town hall* (Casa da Câmara) with its dragon trees is a particularly nice example of Portuguese Renaissance architecture. Built in the 16th century, it has been altered several times over the years. The entrance, above which you can see the country's coat of arms and the royal crown, is on the first floor, and two sets of stairs lead up to it.

From here you have the best view of the pleasant Largo do Pelourinho and next to it the white façade of the parish church of *Nossa Senhora da Piedade* which is decorated with sea-blue *azulejo* tiles. After its construction in the 15th century, this place of worship suffered pirate raids on several occasions. As a result, only the Morgada chapel on the south side is left of the original building. Various master builders in the 17th century gave the church its present Baroque design. The altar painting by German artist Max Römer, who visited Porto Santo in the 1940s, is worth seeing.

CASA COLOMBO – MUSEU DO PORTO SANTO ★ 🌴

The Columbus Museum collects material about seafaring and the history of Porto Santo, and especially about anything connected with the life and the deeds of the famous explorer: ships' models, marine charts, engraved portraits. Columbus is said to have spent some time here in about 1480 as a sugar trader. He married Filipa Moniz, a daughter of Bartolomeu Perestrelo who discovered the island and was the first

Casa Colombo: home, sweet home, but Columbus had bigger fish to fry!

governor of Madeira. The locals like to recount that Christopher Columbus looked out to sea here while living in his father-in-law's house and hatched the first plans for his subsequent crossing of the Atlantic Ocean. The fascinating museum informs you not only about the story of Columbus and his voyages, but also about the age of the Spanish and Portuguese navigators in general. *Closed Mon | admission 2 euros | Travessa da Sacristia 2–4 | museucolombo portosanto.com | ⊙ 30 mins*

EATING & DRINKING

CASA DO VELHO DRAGOEIRO

The owner of this lovely restaurant is a true artist, which is not only reflected in the cosy atmosphere, but mainly in her creative cuisine (for example, the *arroz de marisco*). It is regarded as one of the best restaurants on the island. *Rua Gregório Pestana 16a | tel. 291 634 413 | casadovelhodragoeiro. com | €€*

O FORNO

Visit this rustic grill restaurant if you would like to try top-class meat skewers on Porto Santo. *Av. Henrique Vieira de Castro | tel. 291 984 035 | FB: oforno.oforno.9 | €€*

PÉ NA ÁGUA

Here you are sitting almost literally with one "foot in the water" or at least on the sand! The beach restaurant primarily serves fresh fish, but you can also order a cool beer in the afternoon. In the summer, it is lively here until late into the night, with regular live music and DJ acts. *March–Nov | Sítio das Pedras Pretas | tel. 291 985 242 | penaagua.pt | €€*

SHOPPING

The Rua João Gonçalves Zarco has a number of shops and boutiques, and there's a supermarket *(Pingo Doce)* on the main road *(Av. Dr Manuel Gregório Pestana Jr)*. Next door, the *Centro de Artesanato*, which also houses the tourist information centre, sells miniature windmills, straw hats and various items made from shells.

BEACHES

The golden-yellow sandy beach of ★ ⁂ *Praia do Porto Santo* starts at the harbour and goes all the way to *Ponta da Calheta (▥ U12)*. It is by far the most beautiful beach on the Madeiran archipelago, and is the reason why Porto Santo has evolved into a tourist destination for holidaymakers from Madeira and mainland Portugal. In summer it is crowded with sun-hungry and sand-loving tourists. To the west of Vila Baleira it gets broader, and is then supervised by lifeguards and equipped with toilets, showers (for a charge) and snack bars.

WELLNESS

Porto Santo's sandy beaches give it an advantage over its big green sister. The beaches not only attract bathers to the island, but also hotels which are able to offer thalassotherapy in their spas. The smooth sand was created by ground shells and coral reefs, which

The Praia do Porto Santo is a beach-lover's paradise

were pulverised by the sea. It contains essential minerals with alleged therapeutic effects for orthopaedic and rheumatic conditions. Give it a try, for example at the ☂ *Thalasso Therapy Centre* of the Vila Baleira hotel *(thalasso.vilabaleira.com).*

SPORT & ACTIVITIES

Some people might think that there's nothing to do on Porto Santo other than count the grains of sand, cool off in the water once in a while and perhaps play a little beach volleyball. Others may recall that there is also an 18-hole golf course designed by golf legend Severiano Ballesteros: *Porto Santo Golfe (portosantogolfe.com).*

However, there is much more to explore on the island, particularly in the summer when you can learn

surfing, kite- and windsurfing or stand-up paddle boarding at *On Water Academy (Cabeço da Ponta | mobile 964 838 535 | onwater academy.com).*

Organised tours of the island are available including a jeep safari or explorations on foot at *Lazermar (mobile 963 501 488 | lazermar.com).* Distances are short on Porto Santo so it doesn't take long to change from hiking at the Pico Branco in the island's far northeast to bathing at the Ponta da Calheta at the end of the long sandy beach.

CYCLING

Thanks to the cycle track built parallel to the beach, you can easily cycle around half the island. And if you hire a proper mountain bike, the hilly route round the rest of the island will not be a problem either! Bicycles are available from *Auto Acessórios Colombo | Av. Vieira de Castro 64, Vila Baleira | tel. 291 984 438 | aacolombo. com*

INSIDER TIP
Mountain biking

HIKING

There are two signposted hiking routes: the *Vereda do Pico Branco e Terra Chã* (PR1) will lead you to the northeastern tip of the island with great views (5.4km return trip), and the *Vereda do Pico Castelo* (PR2) will take you on the 4.6km track round the Pico do Facho, the highest peak on the island. From the Pico do Castelo, you have a great view over Vila Baleira and (sometimes) even as far as Madeira.

Historic windmills lend colour to the barren landscape at Portela

HORSE RIDING

At Porto Santo Horseriding Tours, Matias, Isa and their whole team, including the horses, will arrange wonderful tours for everyone, ranging from complete beginners to professional riders. *Portela, near the windmills | mobile 911 798 989*

SCUBA DIVING

Recently, Porto Santo has developed into a paradise for scuba divers: marine life can be observed in the clear and relatively warm water, and wreck diving is an underwater highlight. The recently created artificial reefs at a depth of 30m have already attracted corals and many fish species. Diving sessions, courses and trial courses are offered by *Rhea Dive (in the Vila Baleira Resort | mobile 939 333 777 | rheadive. com)*, among others.

SNORKELLING

If you wish to snorkel in beautiful locations, contact Matias Teixeira at *Porto Santo Destination Tours (mobile 911 798 989 | portosantodestination tours.com)* will take you there. Even though they include the equipment, the tours are free of charge, but Matias would naturally welcome a tip. A special experience is the night-time snorkelling trip (50 euros): you won't believe how much is going on under water in the dark!

NIGHTLIFE

In summer, the beach cafés are transformed into great evening bars. The Caipirinha in the pirate bar *O Corsário Beach Bar (Rua Goulart Medeiros 164 | FB: corsarioportosanto)* is especially delicious, but in the lounge *Bar do*

Henrique (Praia do Ribeiro Cochino | Instagram: bardohenrique) the atmosphere certainly hots up on mild summer evenings. In general, most beach bars are only open in summer when they operate until late at night every single day!

CHALLENGER

You can let off steam all year round dancing to electro, hip hop and other dance music in this club *Fri/Sat 11.30pm–6 am (Sat only in winter) | Rua Estêvão Alencastre | FB: challengerclub1989*

WINE BAR 3 V'S

The cosy wine bar serves its own Porto Santo wine, delicious sangria and tasty *petiscos* – the evenings can extend well into the small hours here. *June–Oct 10pm–2am | Rua Gregório*

Pestana 8 | mobile 917 856 798 | FB: 3vsportosanto

AROUND VILA BALEIRA

🚩 PORTELA
3km / 6 mins by car via the ER111 and ER233

A strong breeze blows across the island of Porto Santo on many days of the year. Centuries ago the inhabitants took advantage of this by building windmills to grind grain, which was then still plentiful on the island. The date of construction of the first mill is a matter of dispute. It is reported that there were 30 *moinhos* on Porto Santo in the early 20th century. By now most of them have become dilapidated, but three old mills have been beautifully restored on the Portela plateau.

A few steps further on, the *Miradouro da Portela* is a fabulous spot for watching the sunset, and there is a suitable restaurant as well: *Panorama Restaurant & Lounge Bar (only in the evening, closed Mon | Estrada Carlos Pestana Vasconcelos | mobile 966 789 680 | panorama-restaurante.pt | €€).* In a cosy and relaxed atmosphere with incredible views, the artistically created dishes taste even better. Make sure that you book early because tables by the window are in high demand. *□ W11*

☑ SERRA DE FORA & SERRA DE DENTRO
5.5km / 10 mins by car to Serra de Fora via the ER223

The lookout point at *Portela* is on the way to the barren landscape of *Serra de Fora* (📖 W11). On the edge of this sleepy hamlet you can decipher a circular stone threshing floor *(aira)*. It is a reminder of the age of the navigators, when Porto Santo supplied grain to Portuguese ships on their voyages to Africa. A "harbour"

INSIDER TIP
Bathe in the harbours

which was suitable for this purpose is *Porto dos Frades*, off the main road, where you will also find a superb bathing spot on the 🏖 *Praia Porto dos Frades*. Serra de Dentro (📖 W10), 2km to the north, lies between the bare cones of the Pico Gandaia, Pico do Cabrito and Pico do Facho, the highest summit (517m) on the island, from where beacon fires once upon a time announced the approach of ships. This part of Porto Santo used to be blessed with the most plentiful water supplies, but today nobody lives in the grey dilapidated houses made of basalt blocks. 📖 W11/W10

☑ CAMACHA
4km / 8 mins by car via the ER111

Camacha (pop. 450) is one of Madeira's centres of grape and wine production. You must visit the small, private ethnographic museum of Senhor Cardina and admire his 1:10 scale models of

INSIDER TIP
Cultural replicas

all listed fountains on the island as well as his replicas of historic tools.

In centuries past, Camacha's residents used the freshwater spring of *Fonte da Areia*, located shortly past the village, as their public laundering place. The water is also said to have healing properties. Today, the "sandy well" is one of the island's ten listed "GEOssítios" due to its unusual geology. 📖 V10

☑ PICO DO CASTELO
4km / 9 mins by car to the miradouro via the ER111

This is what a volcano should look like! The 437-m-high "castle mountain" with its pointed shape is impressive, although the peak of the adjacent Pico do Facho is much less so. At the foot of the volcano, there's a pretty *miradouro*, which is easily accessible by car and from where you have phenomenal views. If you are undeterred by a strenuous ascent via countless steps, you can climb to the volcano's summit: it will take you about half an hour to climb the 180m. Having reached the top, you will see many old walls and a canon, all of which indicate that this site once served as a defensive structure for the local population. 📖 V10

☑ QUINTA DAS PALMEIRAS
5km / 11 mins by car via the ER120

On the island, industrious hands have created a man-made oasis in the middle of the desert. In the little botanical garden, exotic birds flutter and twitter – some flying free, others in cages and on perches. *Daily 10am–5pm | admission 3 euros | Sítio dos Linhares | FB: Quinta Das Palmeiras Mini-Zoo Botânico, Porto Santo | ⏱ 1 hr | 📖 U11*

6 PICO DE ANA FERREIRA

6km / 10 mins by car to the basalt rock face via the ER111

At the northern slope of this hill you can see a beautiful formation of angular basalt columns. Naturally, this impressive "basalt organ" is one of the ten listed GEOssítios of the island. An information board explains its volcanic origin. ▣ *U12*

7 PRAIA DO ZIMBRALINHO 🌴

6km / 11 mins by car via the ER111 and an off-road track

Accessing this dreamlike rocky cove isn't entirely straightforward: shortly before reaching the *Ponta da Calheta* via the ER111, a small road turns off to the right. It then becomes a rough track leading uphill, before making a left-hand turn and, in an arched shape, ending at the *Miradouro das Flores* above the Ponta da Calheta. However, to reach *Praia do Zimbralinho* you ignore that left-hand turning to the viewpoint and instead continue straight ahead until the end of the track. Having parked the car, a footpath leads from here down to the small rocky cove where you can bathe and snorkel in the crystal-clear water. Despite this place no longer being a "secret" beach, when the weather is good there is hardly a better bathing spot on Porto Santo. ▣ *U12*

8 PONTA DA CALHETA

6km / 13 mins by car via the ER111

This is where you reach the end of Porto Santo's beach. Directly off the southwestern tip of the island, looking almost close enough to touch, is the

Quinta das Palmeiras

Ilhéu de Cal with its strangely shaped limestone rocks. On some days a high jet of water spurts out of one of these rocks. The best place to enjoy this spectacle is the *Ponta da Calheta* fish restaurant *(tel. 291 985 322 | FB: pontadacalheta | €€)*.

There is an unimpeded view from the *Miradouro das Flores*, 170m above, across the entire southern part of the island and, weather permitting, even across to Madeira. Not far from here is the *Adega das Levadas (Rua Morenos | tel. 291 982 557 | €–€€)*, a good old-fashioned place to eat meat on the skewer with home-made bread and drink strong *vinho do Porto Santo* produced by the owners themselves. ▣ *U12*

DISCOVERY TOURS

Want to get under the skin of the region? Then our discovery tours provide the perfect guide – they include advice on which sights to visit, tips on where to stop for that perfect holiday snap, a choice of the best places to eat and drink, and suggestions for fun activities.

❶ PICO DO ARIEIRO & PICO RUIVO: MADEIRA'S HIGHEST PEAKS

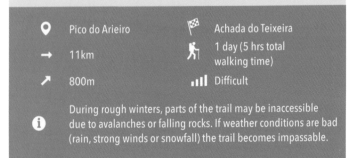

➤ Enjoy the fresh mountain air at 1,800m
➤ Hike from peak to peak on narrow trails
➤ Experience spectacular views into the valleys

📍	Pico do Arieiro	🏁	Achada do Teixeira
→	11km	🚶	1 day (5 hrs total walking time)
↗	800m	📶	Difficult

ℹ️ During rough winters, parts of the trail may be inaccessible due to avalanches or falling rocks. If weather conditions are bad (rain, strong winds or snowfall) the trail becomes impassable.

Lookout point on Pico do Arieiro

THE MOUNTAINS ARE CALLING!

And impressive mountains they are! Put on your walking boots and set out for the ★ *hike to the two peaks!* Although demanding, in good weather this tour is beautiful, but you need to be an early bird. It starts first thing in the morning at the car park of Madeira's third-highest peak, the ❶ Pico do Arieiro ➤ p. 85. There is no public transport here, which is why you will need another means of transportation to get to the starting point (e.g. a taxi: the ride from Funchal to the Pico do Arieiro or from Achada do Teixeira back to Funchal including waiting time costs 120 euros). To return to your hotel, you need to book a taxi for pickup at the Achada do Teixeira car park in advance *(Santana taxi rank: tel. 291 572 540)*.

From 9am, the Achada do Teixeira car park starts to fill up with tourist coaches and hire cars. If you come early, you can enjoy the wonderful atmosphere high above the valleys while the morning fog slowly reveals the mountain peaks: absolutely magical! Initially, you walk past the controversial NATO listening station and the tourist information centre with a souvenir shop, café and loos

INSIDER TIP
The Arieiro fog

❶ Pico do Arieiro

900m 20 mins

and *climb a few steps* to the peak of the Arieiro. The breathtaking panorama of Madeira's mountains will quickly make you forget the modern buildings below.

A SHORTCUT TO HEAVEN

Follow the red and yellow trail markers. At first, the trail is fairly wide and there are some railings to help you along. After about 15 minutes, you will reach a rocky peak known as ❷ Ninho da Manta ("buzzard's nest") where you will find the first lookout point. This part of the trail is also easily accessible for less experienced hikers. In order to get to the second ❸ Miradouro with its table made of tuff rock, the so-called Pedra Rija, you will have to *cross a small narrow ridge.* The steps seem to lead straight into the sky, which is why many hikers name their ultimate Instagram picture taken here as "Stairway to Heaven".

❷ Ninho da Manta

| 350m | 10 mins |

❸ Miradouro

| 650m | 20 mins |

❹ Pico do Gato

The route now makes a steep but secure lateral descent along the rock walls of the Pico do Cidrão (1,798m) *down countless steps and through a gap in the rocks to the foot of the* ❹ Pico do Gato (1,780m). Tree heath and gorse line the path before it is swallowed by the first tunnel. When the trail branches at the end of the tunnel, *take the easier route to the left,* where beautiful views into the Valley of the Nuns and four more tunnels await you.

| 3km | 1½ hrs |

When both paths reunite, the terrain becomes much more difficult. Following a mountain slide, a part of the path was resurfaced, but there is still a section of around 30m which is rough and slightly narrower. Once this point has been passed, the only existing path lined with tree heathland ascends continually, first gently and then in hairpin bends. The path ascending from

Achada do Teixeira meets this path on the right-hand side and the *ascending path straight ahead* leads to the ⑤ Pico Ruivo refuge, which is easy to see. Here you can buy a snack or have your own picnic. The walls are a good place for a midday rest.

⑤ Pico Ruivo refuge

500m   20 mins

TO THE SUMMIT & BACK

All refreshed, it is time to tackle the summit. *Go up a few stone steps leading to the left. When the path forks, take the left-hand path* (the path to the right leads to the Encumeada Pass). In less than half an hour, you will be standing on top of the ⑥ Pico Ruivo ➤ p. 84 (1,862m), Madeira's highest peak. In clear weather, you will be rewarded with a magnificent panoramic view of the Paúl da Serra plateau, the mountain peaks around the Curral das Freiras and Madeira's north coast. You might even be able to spot the island of Porto Santo and the Ponta de São Lourenço.

⑥ Pico Ruivo

5.5km   2½ hrs

To hike back, *you will initially follow the same trail back to* the Pico Ruivo refuge. Shortly thereafter, take *the path that forks to the left in the direction of Achada do Teixeira*. This path with its many stone slabs gently

En route to the island's highest peak

descends the mountain. When you reach the path heading to Ilha, ignore it and *continue straight ahead*. In less than an hour, you should reach the car park at the back of the ❼ Achada do Teixeira ridge.

❼ Achada do Teixeira

❷ BOCA DO RISCO – PANORAMIC VIEW OF THE NORTH COAST

➤ Follow the *levada* in the Machico valley
➤ Pass through the "Dangerous Mouth" to reach the north coast
➤ Take the adventurous coastal trail towards Porto da Cruz

📍	Caniçal Tunnel	🏁	Porto da Cruz
→	13.5km	🥾	4 hrs (3 hrs total walking time)
↗	380m		
▁▃▅	Medium		

ℹ️ Do not attempt the hike up the narrow coastal path on the north side if you are not sure-footed or good with heights. If weather conditions are bad (rain, strong winds or snowfall) the trail becomes impassable.

THE WINE CARRIERS' ARTERY

For centuries, the *Borracheiros*, as the wine carriers were called, who could be a little drunk at times, used the pass between Machico and Porto da Cruz because it was the shortest route. It is difficult to imagine today how they managed this precarious cliff-side walk, somewhat tipsy, while carrying wineskins made from goats.

After reaching the starting point *(bus 113 from Funchal or Machico to the old Caniçal tunnel (stop "Pico do Facho"): Mon-Fri 7-9am 4 buses, Sat 3 buses, Sun 2 buses | return ticket 6 euros)*, the walk starts in an easy manner. Look for the little house on the left-hand side of the road at the western entrance of the old **❶ Caniçal tunnel** on the outskirts of Machico ➤ p. 96. The Levada do Caniçal begins right in front of it. *At first you walk along a paved road, but before long it turns into a narrow path across the fields.* Enjoy the beautiful view of the valley of Machico and the Pico do Facho straight ahead before you enter the small wood. On the other side you'll come to a wide-open view of terraced plots bearing bananas, wine grapes and vegetables. Here, the farmers use imaginative scarecrows to protect their crop.

❶ Caniçal tunnel

45km 1 day

ADEUS, LEVADA!

After passing through a gap in the rocks, the levada bends slightly to the right into a deep-cut little valley. Follow the trail along the stream until you see two steps leading to a fork on the right – take this path to Boca do Risco. The stone-studded trail gently ascends before dropping back down into a valley where it crosses through pine forest and more terraced fields. Towards the end, the trails becomes ever steeper until, after about 1½ hours and a slight bend to the left, you will

Boca do Risco: when you realise the climb has been worth the effort

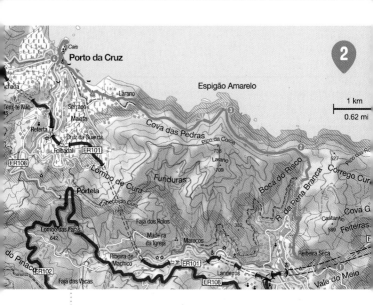

1 km
0.62 mi

---

② Boca do Risco

2.5km   35 mins

③ Ponta do Espigão Amarelo

reach the rocky pass known as **② Boca do Risco**. From a height of about 360m, the view stretches out over the eastern side of the rugged, largely unspoilt north coast. Up here on the pass it is windy, and a few metres between the protected and exposed areas make all the difference. Despite the excellent views, it is generally too blowy for a break here, and in stormy conditions you know why this spot is known as the "dangerous opening".

VIEW OF EAGLE ROCK FROM THE YELLOW SPIKE
A dense cover of tree heath and shrubs close in on the trail as it climbs on towards the west. This section is one of the most spectacular trails on Madeira. Light often breaks through the jungle-like greenery where the vegetation becomes sparser as the trail crosses more exposed terrain. Before long, the trail comes to a rock wall where it becomes steep and narrow with loose gravel. There is usually a wire rope handrail provided for particularly difficult sections of the trail. If the wire is broken or missing, you must be extremely careful and sure-footed. A knee-high mile marker identifies the headland known as **③ Ponta do Espigão Amarelo**.

This lookout point offers a brilliant view of Penha de Águia (Eagle Rock) and neighbouring Porto da Cruz.

At this point, you have conquered more than half the trail and its most difficult sections are behind you. The landscape begins to change once again as eucalyptus and pine trees rise up on the slopes around you. *A few stone steps take you down* to a deeply cut water channel and through two other similar little gorges. Shortly thereafter you will see a dirt road. At a mostly steady elevation, it leads to a gap and to the left into a valley with terraced plots. *The trail continues along a mountain ridge* running parallel to the coast, accompanied by a water channel. You will soon come across the first houses of Larano as you reach the tarmac road. *Follow the road steeply downhill for about 1km until you reach a small hill. Just before the hill a concrete driveway with letterboxes branches off sharply to the right. On the left side of the driveway, steps lead down to a clearly visible levada path. Follow this path past fields of vegetables and cross over a dirt track. When you see a stable built into the rocks, turn left and head on towards the sea.*

6.5km   1½ hrs

TOWARDS THE SEA

The trail begins to descend steeply once again over a small ridge, through a dry (only in summer) stream bed and right across the cliff towards a group of houses. Head down the steps that you will find above the houses. Keep to the left as you continue over the hill until you reach a paved path. A stone wall marks the fork to the right that leads towards the coast. After you walk around a stream bed with a collapsed bridge, the trail continues directly alongside the sea. Shortly thereafter you will come across the coastal path to ❹ Porto da Cruz ➤ p. 87. It will bring you to the cafés on the seaside promenade, the saltwater swimming pool *(only in summer | 2 euros),* where you can enjoy a refreshing dip, and the small harbour. Head up to the left to reach the church and the bus station *(bus 53 to Machico or Funchal: Mon–Fri from 1pm 4 buses, Sat only 3.50pm and 5.55pm, Sun only 10.25am).*

❹ Porto da Cruz

❸ RABAÇAL: A WILDERNESS OF MAGICAL WATERS

➤ Hike through thick laurel forests
➤ Admire breathtaking waterfalls
➤ Take a break in the Rabaçal forester's lodge

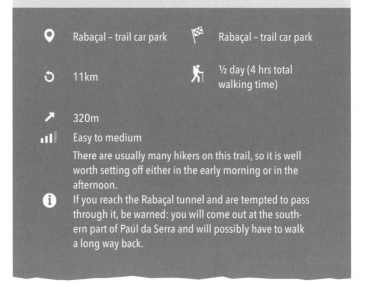

📍 Rabaçal – trail car park

🏁 Rabaçal – trail car park

🔄 11km

🏃 ½ day (4 hrs total walking time)

↗ 320m

📶 Easy to medium

There are usually many hikers on this trail, so it is well worth setting off either in the early morning or in the afternoon.

ℹ If you reach the Rabaçal tunnel and are tempted to pass through it, be warned: you will come out at the southern part of Paúl da Serra and will possibly have to walk a long way back.

BRAVE IT TO THE WATERFALLS

Cascata do Risco and 25 Fontes are the two most beautiful and popular attractions in Rabaçal. You can reach both by walking a short circuit of the area. Start off at the ❶ Rabaçal trail car park located on the road coming from Paúl da Serra. *From the car park, follow the paved road (cars are prohibited) for about 30 minutes downhill to the* ❷ Rabaçal forester's lodge *(shuttle bus ticket 3 euros or return ticket 5 euros).* The trails are well signposted. *Take the wide, level path signed to* ❸ Levada do Risco. *Shortly after, where a fork in the road leads to the levada of the 25 Springs, stay on the trail going along the Levada do Risco for about another 15 minutes until a secured path branches off to the right.* It leads to the basin of the ❹ Cascata do Risco before ending at a **⑤ Lookout Point**. The veil of water cascading down the 100-m-high rock wall at the first stop of this tour is truly amazing.

FOLLOW THE LEVADA

Retrace your steps. There is no point in going underneath the waterfall and through the tunnel because the trail has been closed for safety reasons just a few metres further on. *Once you've reached the crossroads with the fork leading to the 25 Springs, take a right turn.* Stone steps, hairpin bends and a second set of steps bring you to **⑥ Levada das 25 Fontes**. *Follow the levada against the current.* Before long you will find a lookout point on the right from which you can see the continuing path of the *levada* and the valley below.

At the point where the *levada* disappears into the mountain, stone steps with wooden railings lead to a *bridge that will take you back up to the levada.* Just a little further on, you can gaze down into the Risco basin. *Follow the levada wall out over the cliff, which is only secured by tree heath and has been turned into a*

| 1km | 30 mins |

⑤ Lookout Point

| 1km | 30mins |

⑥ Levada das 25 Fontes

| 2.5km | 1 day |

A magical spot: 25 springs feed the Lagoa das 25 Fontes

one-way section of the trail, as far as the plateau where the path curves to the right down into the valley of the 25 Springs. From here, the trail goes straight on as it descends to the Levada da Rocha Vermelha. *Don't take this path. Instead, follow the stream's current until you reach a second bridge where you bear to the right to follow the wider levada.*

25 REASONS FOR A PICNIC

After a few more metres, the valley basin will open up to reveal the **7 25 Fontes**. In dry summer months, the water only seems to trickle over the rocks, if at all. However, during the rest of the year you can expect to see water cascading down from the springs. Now you can enjoy your well-earned picnic lunch and the incredible mixture of water and lush vegetation or cool your feet in the lake.

7 25 Fontes

2.5km   1 day

8 Levada do Risco

2km   40 mins

1 Rabaçal

Retrace your steps: turn left onto a bypass which leads uphill on stone steps and then downhill until you get back to the Levada das 25 Fontes, following the direction of the current and ignoring the branch to the forester's lodge. The path leads through a narrow rock gap, followed shortly after by a set of steps made of red tuff rock. The steps wind up to the left to the **8 Levada do Risco**. *There are more steps to climb after you cross the* levada *until you reach the courtyard in front of the loos at Rabaçal house.* Have a break in the **Café Rabaçal Nature Spot** (daily 9am–6pm, in winter until 5pm | mobile 963 797 356). Go past the house to get onto the paved road that leads back to the trail car park in **1 Rabaçal**.

④ THE SOUTHWEST: MADEIRA'S SUNNY SIDE

➤ Steep banana terraces and pretty villages
➤ Car wash under a waterfall
➤ Bathing break on a sandy beach

📍 Ribeira Brava

🏁 Porto Moniz

→ approx. 72km

🚗 ½ day (2 hrs total driving time)

ℹ The old coastal roads are often narrow and run close to the edge of the steep cliffs. In rainy winter weather, falling rocks may block the roads.

INTO THE SUN

Madeira's sunny southwest is omitted from many round trips, which is a shame. Don't make that mistake! Start off in the morning from ❶ Ribeira Brava ➤ p. 63, a bustling commercial town located at the mouth of its namesake river. After a short stroll through the market, a sweet treat in one of the Pastelarias on the harbour promenade and a visit to the Baroque church of São Bento, it's time to *head west*. Unfortunately, the first 3km of the coastal road are impassable, so you will have to *drive back towards the motorway for just a bit. At the roundabout leaving town, take the exit for the tunnel, heading towards Ponta do Sol/Calheta (VR3).* You will pass through the banana plantations of Lugar de Baixo. Over the last few years this town has sadly become known for its poorly constructed marina. Although the sea has scraped away at much of the concrete, the half-finished ruins are still an eyesore. After passing through another tunnel, you will arrive in the pretty little town of ❷ Ponta do Sol ➤ p. 62. *At this point you will leave the motorway and take the old regional road ER101 that runs right along the sea. To do so, exit the roundabout in Ponta do Sol to the left in the direction of*

❶ Ribeira Brava

5.5km   25 mins

❷ Ponta do Sol

4.5km   5 mins

You can't escape the bananas in Madalena do Mar

the church. It is well worth taking a short break here to walk through the lovingly restored town centre.

LIE IN AFRICAN SAND

The next section of the road is definitely one of the most spectacular on the island: sometimes you'll even get a free car wash under one of the waterfalls.

INSIDER TIP
Waterfall car wash

❸ Madalena do Mar ➤ p. 64 lives mostly from the cultivation of bananas, so you'll see banana plants covering every last square metre. *Calheta is the next destination. When the motorway (VR3) divides, take the old regional road (ER101),* which leads directly to ❹ Praia da Calheta ➤ p. 67. This is the perfect place for a swim. The golden sand was shipped in especially from Africa so that a beach could be made on the southwest coast. It is also worth touring the old sugar-cane mill. Calheta is still one of the most important sugar cane-growing regions on Madeira; today most of the sugar is used to make *aguardente* for *poncha*.

After Calheta, the regional road ER 222/223 winds through Estreito da Calheta, which sits at a slightly higher elevation, before heading back down to the sea. Surfers flock to ❺ Jardim do Mar ➤ p. 67 for the island's best, but also most challenging waves. The town has a real surfing vibe with its lounge-style cafés

❸ Madalena do Mar

5km · 10 mins

❹ Praia da Calheta

11km · 15 mins

❺ Jardim do Mar

3.5km · 5 mins

such as Joe's Bar ➤ p. 67. *A long tunnel* links Jardim do Mar with the fishing village of ❻ Paúl do Mar ➤ p. 68. The Bay Side restaurant *(Rua do Cais 12 | Tel. 2 91 87 20 22 | €)* at the fishing harbour has sea views and is a great place to stop for lunch.

UP THE WINDING ROAD

A steep, winding road snakes its way from the western edge of town up to ❼ Fajã da Ovelha ➤ p. 71. From here, the route leaves the coast to curve through many of the towns and villages located up on the plateaus before finally reaching Madeira's westernmost town, ❽ Ponta do Pargo ➤ p. 70. The lighthouse on the western point juts out impressively from the coast. You may want to take a few photographs before getting back into the car to *head along the winding ER101.*

In ❾ Achadas da Cruz ➤ p. 71 a *cable car (return ticket 3 euros, last ride in summer 8pm, in winter 6pm)*

INSIDER TIP
Sunset at land's end

) connects the town with the fields on the fajã down at the coast. It is particularly romantic to watch the sunset from the *fajã,* but don't miss the last return ride of the day.

Shortly after you get *back on the main road* it will merge with the ER110 coming from Paúl da Serra. *The route heads straight on,* past Santa with its lovely lookout point, back down to ❿ Porto Moniz ➤ p. 76. This is the last stop of the tour. If you feel like it, you can take a refreshing dip in the local saltwater swimming pool or call it a day and enjoy a large plate of *lapas grelhadas* (grilled limpets) in one of the restaurants.

❻ Paúl do Mar	
❼ Fajã da Ovelha	
11.5km 10 mins	
❽ Ponta do Pargo	
13.5km 30 mins	
❾ Achadas da Cruz	
12km 15 mins	
❿ Porto Moniz	

GOOD TO KNOW

HOLIDAY BASICS

ARRIVAL

GETTING THERE

You get to Madeira either by cruise liner (in which case you usually won't be staying long) or by plane. Recently, a ferry connection (Canaries–Madeira–Algarve, *madeira-ferry.pt*) has been reintroduced, but it only sails on a few dates in summer. Package holidays with a flight and accommodation are the simplest and generally the cheapest way to go to Madeira. A charter flight from Western Europe in summer without hotel costs 300–400 euros. The prices are slightly cheaper for TAP Portugal's scheduled flights, which go several times daily – but you have to change in Lisbon. In summer TAP also flies several times a week from Lisbon direct to Porto Santo. Otherwise, you can get there from Madeira by ferry from Funchal *(portosantoline.pt)* or by Binter turbo-prop aircraft *(bintercanarias.com)* from the Cristiano Ronaldo Airport.

Madeira's airport, renamed after the footballer, is located some 20km east of Funchal. Please note that despite the extension of the runway, difficult cross-wind conditions along the cliff coast can make it impossible to land there. The best option is then to land on Porto Santo and take the

RESPONSIBLE TRAVEL

Are you aware of your carbon footprint while travelling? You can offset your emissions *(myclimate.org)*, plan your route with the environment in mind *(routerank.com)* and go gently on both nature and culture. If you would like to find out more about ecotourism please visit: *ecotourism.org*.

Azulejo tiles at the Chamber of Commerce in Funchal

ferry to Madeira, but frequently the plane will fly back to Lisbon and attempt a new landing the next day.

GETTING IN

If you are travelling from the UK, you will need a passport that was issued less than 10 years before the date you enter Portugal (check the "date of issue"). It must also be valid for at least three months after the date you intend to leave Portugal (check the "expiry date"). Citizens of the US or Canada currently require a visa only if staying for longer than three months. All children must travel with their own passports.

CLIMATE & WHEN TO GO

Madeira enjoys a mild climate all year round. Even in January and February it is exceptional for the daytime temperature on the south coast to fall below 15°C. The warmest months are July, August and September, when the thermometer can rise to more than 25°C on the south coast.

The weather on Madeira can be extremely changeable, and can differ from one place to another at any one time. In winter and spring, in particular, you need to expect the odd shower or even a storm. In general, weather charts and apps only apply to Funchal, and webcams may be more helpful for planning your day. Please note as a rule of thumb: when the trade winds blow from the northeast, it is often cloudy in the mountains and on the north coast, but stable. A southeast wind *(leste)* from the Sahara means warm and sunny weather for most of the island. Westerly winds cause changeable and rainy weather, as they carry alternating fronts of warm and cold air. The best rule of all is probably: if you don't like the weather, drive to the other side of the island!

GETTING AROUND

BUS

The *Aerobus (5 euros | samt.pt)* takes you from the airport to Funchal's hotel quarter (departure in front of the arrival hall). Almost any place on Madeira and the great majority of sights (with the exception of the mountain regions) can be reached by bus, although the journey may be laborious.

Madeira has no unified bus network. Instead, a number of bus operators are responsible for different regions. In the Funchal area the bus company is *Horários do Funchal (horariosdofunchal.pt, with bus timetable for the Funchal region)*. *EACL (eacl.pt)* links the island's capital to Caniço, *Rodoeste (rodoeste.pt)* has the routes to the west of Madeira, and *SAM (sam.pt)* covers the east. There is a kind of central bus station on the edge of the old quarter of Funchal: most buses depart between the cablecar terminus and Praça da Autonomia. Others stop along the Avenida do

Mar, as do many private hotel shuttle buses.

Bus tickets can normally be purchased directly from the driver. In Funchal it is cheaper to buy a rechargeable "giro" card (0.50 euros plus the ticket price). Multi-day tickets are also available (e.g. 21.50 euros for 7 days).

INSIDER TIP
Funchal at a flat rate

CAR HIRE

National and international car hire firms have offices at the airports, in the capitals of Madeira and Porto Santo and in Caniço de Baixo. Local operators tempt visitors with special offers, but it is certainly worth comparing their prices with offers available when booking at home. Drivers of hire cars must be at least 21 years old. In most cases, you will need a credit card to hire a car. Car rental costs between 25 and 70 euros per day, with unlimited mileage. Make sure that the brakes on your car work well and that it has sufficient horsepower to master the steep slopes of the island's mountains.

DRIVING ON MADEIRA

The speed limit on Madeira is 50kmh in towns, 90kmh on country roads, and 100kmh on the *via rápida*, Madeira's fast highway. The legal limit of blood-alcohol is 0.5g/litre and the use of seat belts is obligatory. In case of a breakdown, drivers leaving the vehicle must wear a high-vis jacket. The main roads on Madeira and Porto Santo are surfaced with asphalt and are generally in good condition; many of them now run through tunnels.

FESTIVALS & EVENTS
ALL YEAR ROUND

FEBRUARY
Carnival (Funchal)

APRIL/MAY
⭐ **Festa da Flor** (Funchal): Procession through the streets (photo) with floats decorated with flowers.

MAY
Fica na Cidade (Funchal): Open-air music festival (free) in various locations. FB: ficanacidade
Maktub Soundsgood Festival (Paúl do Mar): Reggae festival

JUNE
Festival do Atlântico (Funchal): Concerts, street musicians and (every Saturday evening) a fireworks competition and concert in the harbour.

JULY
Nos Summer Opening (Parque de Santa Catarina, Funchal): Music festival featuring rock, hip-hop, reggae. *nossummeropening.com*

AUGUST
Nossa Senhora do Monte (Monte): Pilgrimage on the day of the Assumption of the Virgin.

SEPTEMBER
Madeira Wine festival (Funchal, Estreito de Câmara de Lobos)
Festival Colombo: (Porto Santo, Vila Baleira): Medieval market and a historical parade.

OCTOBER/NOVEMBER/ DECEMBER
Festival da Natureza: Over a week in early October, Madeira celebrates nature – its most valuable treasure.
Festa do Senhor dos Milagres (Machico, 9 October): Night-time procession in honour of a miracle-working image of Jesus.
Chestnut Festival (Curral das Freiras, around 1 November)
Fim do Ano (Funchal): The end of the old year begins in late November. The climax is New Year's Eve, when the famous fireworks are set off in the bay.

Exercise extreme caution when driving on mountain roads in heavy rain. Stones and debris often roll down the slopes onto the road, and roads are sometimes closed *(prociv madeira.pt)*. Drive carefully in fog in the highlands as cows on the road are often quite difficult to see from a distance. Parking spaces in the centre of Funchal are scarce and chargeable.

TAXI

The taxi rank is at the *Praças de Taxi* and all taxis have a meter for journeys within Funchal and a copy of the tariff for reference. The minimum fare is 2.50 euros *(Mon–Fri 7am–10pm)*. To call a taxi in Funchal dial *tel. 291 764 476* or ask the hotel reception. For tours of the island, the price should be approx. 120 euros. Trips to and from the airport cost 30–70 euros, depending on the distance. Overland journeys are charged according to a list of fixed prices, even though the meter is not switched on.

EMERGENCIES

CONSULATES & EMBASSIES

British Honorary Consulate: *Av de Zarco 2, Funchal | tel. 291 212 860 | email: brit.confunchal@mail.eunet.pt*
US Embassy in Lisbon: *US citizens should contact the embassy in Lisbon, pt.usembassy.gov*

EMERGENCY SERVICES

For police, fire brigade and ambulance: tel. 112

Mountain rescue (Protecção Civil): tel. 291 700 112
SANAS sea rescue: tel. 291 230 112

HEALTH

Before you travel, take out international health insurance. Many hotels can call a hotel doctor in an emergency. You'll need to pay immediately, get a receipt and then present your bills to your insurance company for a refund. EU citizens can recoup the costs at home by producing an invoice.

There are enough pharmacies, at least in the towns *(farmácias, postos de medicamentos)*, and one of them is always open. The current rota is displayed on the door of every pharmacy. You can find a list of contact addresses at *www.sesaram.pt.*

ESSENTIALS

ACCOMMODATION

Madeira offers all kinds of accommodation: from a campsites, glamping, hostels and cheap B&Bs to 5-star luxury hotels. There will be something for all budgets and preferences. The restored *quintas* are particularly beautiful (see p. 22).

BEACHES & BATHING

Madeira is not an island of beaches. In Calheta and Machico artificial beaches were created, and at Prainha as well as in Seixal you will find short stretches of black sand. Otherwise, there are hotel pools, coarse pebble beaches and countless rocks which, in some places and with the help of concrete, have been turned into fabulous bathing complexes (e.g. in Porto Moniz). If you are looking for a real bathing holiday, Porto Santo with its 9-km-long sandy beach is better suited than Madeira.

There are no nudist beaches on the archipelago. Topless bathing is only acceptable around a hotel pool, if at all; in public pools and on the beach it is considered offensive.

HOW MUCH DOES IT COST?

Poncha	2–3 euros for a mini-cocktail
Bica	80 cents for an espresso
Lapas	8 euros for a serving of limpets
Petrol	1.50 euros for 1 litre of unleaded
Public pool	2–4 euros per day at the seawater pool
Souvenir	18–25 euros for a bottle of Madeira wine (aged for 10 years)

CUSTOMS

Within the European Union goods for personal use can be imported and exported duty-free. However, please note that some limits should not be exceeded, e.g. 800 cigarettes, 10 litres of spirits per person (over the age of 17). However, if travelling from the UK and other non-EU countries you will need to check your allowances before bringing things in or out of the country. When flying into Portuigal, non-EU citizens require an onward or return ticket.

DRINKING WATER

The tap water is safe to drink but tastes slightly chlorinated and has often been chemically treated. There is no reason not to use it for cleaning your teeth, but it is advisable to buy drinking water in a supermarket, e.g. as a 5-litre canister.

INFORMATION

The official tourist information portal *visitmadeira.com* can provide a lot of information in advance. Furthermore, the tourist information offices (*Posto de Turismo*) in the centre of all major villages and towns, for example in Funchal in the *Av. Arriaga 16 | tel. 291 211 902*, have town maps and hiking brochures.

LANGUAGE

The people of Madeira speak Portuguese with their own dialect, which the mainland Portuguese recognise at once. Visitors to the island can get by very well speaking English. In hotels, restaurants and agencies the staff have often been trained at the school of tourism to look after foreign visitors and may be fluent in more than one foreign language. Anyone who would like to learn Portuguese on Madeira can book an individual language course, e.g. at the *Academia de Línguas da Madeira (alm-madeira. com)*.

MONEY

Cash machines (ATMs, *multibancos*) can be found almost everywhere. The amount that can be withdrawn is limited to two times 200 euros daily, and your bank may charge you for withdrawals. The cash machines of ATM Euronet Worldwide don't have any withdrawal limit. Payment by credit card or EC cheque card is accepted by hire car companies as well as in almost all hotels, restaurants and shops.

OPENING HOURS

Tourist information offices, small shops and public institutions are normally open Monday–Friday 9am–12.30pm and 2.30-6pm, Saturday 9am-1pm. Museums are often closed on Mondays. Banks open Monday–Friday 9am–3pm. As a rule, supermarkets and shopping centres are open daily until 10pm without a midday break.

Unless otherwise shown, the restaurants described in this guide are open daily noon-3pm and from 6pm (usually until approx. 11pm). Evening shopping is possible in shopping centres *(e.g. Madeira Shopping and Forum Madeira)* until 11pm, and at the weekend until midnight.

POST

A red and white sign with a horse rider and the letters CTT identifies post offices. Their usual hours are Monday–Friday 9am-6pm. Stamps *(selos)* are also on sale in licensed bars, newsagents and kiosks. Postcards and letters up to 20g within Europe need a 0.86 euro stamp.

PRICES

Museum admission costs up to 10 euros, with concessions (mostly 50%) for children, students and pensioners. ☛ On some Sunday mornings, admission is free, and some museums in Funchal are always freely accessible. There are some places (e.g. Skywalk at the Cabo Girão, trout farm in Ribeiro Frio), which are supposed to charge admission fees, but these had not been set by the time this guide went to press.

PUBLIC HOLIDAYS

1 Jan	Ano Novo (New Year's Day)
Feb/March	Carnival (Shrove Tuesday)
March/April	Sextafeira Santa (Good Friday)
25 April	Dia da Libertade (Day of the Carnation Revolution, 1974)
1 May	Dia do Trabalhor (Labour Day)
May/June	Corpo de Deus (Corpus Christi)
10 June	Dia de Portugal (in honour of national poet Luís Vaz de Camões)
15 Aug	Assunção (Assumption Day)
5 Oct	Implantação da República (Foundation of the Republic, 1910)
1 Nov	Todos os Santos (All Saints' Day)
1 Dec	Restauração da Independência (end of the union with Spain, 1640)
8 Dec	Imaculada Conceição (Immaculate Conception)
25 Dec	Natal (Christmas)

TELEPHONE & WIFI

The country code for Portugal (including Madeira and Porto Santo) is 351 followed by the full telephone number. Mobile numbers on Madeira begin with a "9" and landline numbers with a "2".

When making a call from Madeira,

dial 0044 for the UK; 00353 for Ireland; 001 for the US and Canada; 0061 for Australia; then dial the local code without "0" and then the individual number.

Most hotels offer free Wi-Fi, at least in the lobby. WiFi is also available in almost all restaurants and cafés.

TIPPING

In restaurants the amount on the bill is usually rounded up or 5–10 per cent of the sum is added as a tip. Simply leave your tip on the plate on which the bill is brought. It is not customary to ask the waiter to charge a rounded-up amount when paying your bill.

Taxi drivers, chambermaids, porters, tour guides and shoe cleaners are also pleased to receive a top-up to their usually low wages.

TOILETS

Because of the post-war plumbing when narrow pipes were used, many of the older-type loos and those in rustic bars (especially in the mountains) cannot take toilet tissue. Therefore, please throw it in the provided bin.

WEATHER IN FUNCHAL

High season
Low season

	JAN	FEB	MARCH	APRIL	MAY	JUNE	JULY	AUG	SEPT	OCT	NOV	DEC
Daytime temperatures	14°	14°	16°	18°	21°	25°	28°	28°	26°	22°	18°	14°
Night-time temperatures	7°	7°	9°	11°	13°	17°	20°	20°	19°	15°	11°	9°
Hours of sunshine per day	5	5	6	8	10	10	12	10	8	6	5	4
Rainfall days per month	9	8	8	7	5	3	1	3	6	11	9	12
Water temperature in °C	14	13	14	14	17	20	23	25	23	21	18	15

☀ Hours of sunshine per day   🌂 Rainfall days per month   ≈ Water temperature in °C

WORDS & PHRASES
IN PORTUGUESE

SMALLTALK

yes/no/maybe	*sim/não/talvez*
please	*se faz favor*
thank you	*obrigado (m)/obrigada (f)*
Good morning/evening/night	*Bom dia!/Boa tarde!/Boa noite!*
Hello/goodbye!	*Olá!/Cião!*
My name is ...	*Chamo-me …*
What is your name?	*Como te chamas? (informal)/Como se chama? (formal)*
I am from ...	*Sou de …*
Sorry!	*Desculpa! (informal)/Desculpe! (formal)*
Pardon?	*Como?*
I (don't) like this	*(Não) Gosto disto.*
good/bad	*bem/mal*

SYMBOLS

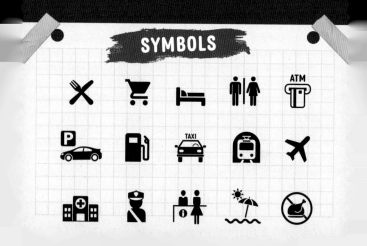

EATING & DRINKING

The menu, please!	*A ementa, se faz favor.*
bottle/glass	*garrafa/copo*
salt/pepper/sugar	*sal/pimenta/açúcar*
vinegar/oil	*vinagre/azeite*
knife/fork/spoon	*faca/garfo/colher*
milk/cream/lemon	*leite/nata/limão*
with/without ice/sparkling/still	*com/sem gelo/ com gás / sem gás*
vegetarian/allergy	*vegetariano, -a/alergia*
bill	*conta*
The bill, please.	*A conta, se faz favor.*
cash/credit card	*em dinheiro/com cartão de crédito*

MISCELLANEOUS

Where is …?/Where are …?	*Onde é …?/Onde são …?*
What time is it?	*Que horas são?*
It's three o'clock.	*São três horas.*
today/tomorrow/yesterday	*hoje/amanhã/ontem*
How much is …?	*Quanto custa …?*
Where can I access the Internet?	*Onde há acesso à internet?*
Help!/Look out!	*Socorro!/Atenção!*
fever/pain	*febre/dores*
pharmacy/drug store	*farmácia/drogaria*
ban/prohibited	*interdição/proibido*
broken/it's not working	*estragado/não funciona*
breakdown/garage	*avaria/garagem*
timetable/ticket	*horário/bilhete*
0/1/2/3/4/5/6/7/8/9/ 10/100/1000	*zero/um, uma/dois, duas/ três/quatro/cinco/seis/ sete/oito/nove/dez/ cem/ mil*

HOLIDAY VIBES

FOR RELAXATION & CHILLING

FOR BOOKWORMS & FILM BUFFS

📖 THE DEVIL ON HER TONGUE

Linda Holeman's novel tells the gripping story of Diamantina who, in the middle of the 18th century, escapes poverty, marries a winegrower, comes to Madeira and experiences her marriage as a prison. (2015)

📖 BREATH OF SUSPICION/ SKELETON STAFF/WITNESS BEFORE THE FACT

Three novels set on Madeira by master crime writer Elizabeth Ferrars. Currently only available on Kindle as part of The Murder Room series.

🎥 RONALDO

Filmed over a period of 14 months, this documentary tells the story of how Cristiano Ronaldo dos Santos Aveiro became the world-class footballer CR7. You will learn that there is something else that matters in the life of the ambitious striker: his family. (2015, director: Anthony Wonke)

PLAYLIST

0:58

‖ JESUS OR A GUN – FLY HIGH
Successful debut single by the island's latest rock band.

▶ CRISTINA BRANCO – AULA DE NATAÇÃO
The video accompanying the *fado* song about the "swimming lesson" is set in Ponta do Sol.

▶ SÉTIMA LEGIÃO – SETE MARES
The legendary band, founded by Madeiran Ricardo Camacho, sings of the seven seas.

▶ AMÁLIA RODRIGUES – BAILINHO DA MADEIRA
The Queen of Fado sings about the "Garden in the Atlantic".

▶ XUTOS & PONTAPÉS – HOMEM DO LEME
Madeira's most loved rock band has produced this homage to the "man at the helm".

Your holiday soundtrack can be found on **Spotify** under **MARCO POLO Portugal**

Or scan this code with the Spotify app

ONLINE

MADEIRAISLANDNEWS.COM
British blogger Tobi who lives on Madeira posts interesting articles on current island affairs, and doesn't shy away from criticising certain events.

LOBOSONDA.COM
What are the whales up to? This blog is by the whale-watching teams of Lobosonda, from Calheta, who are keen on sustainability. It features regular reports on boat trips and whale sightings.

DANISHOME.CH
Enjoying Madeira in 1967. A British couple has recorded their trip to sunny Madeira on 8mm film. Watch Funchal, market scenes, mountain roads and the locals with a nostalgic tint.

NETMADEIRA.COM
If you want to know what the weather is like in the mountains or on the other side of the island, just watch the webcam footage. You will see immediately whether it's worth setting off for a hike

TRAVEL PURSUIT

THE MARCO POLO HOLIDAY QUIZ

Do you know your facts about Madeira? Here you can test your knowledge of the little secrets and idiosyncrasies of the island and its people. You will find the correct answers at the bottom of this page and in detail on pages 18 to 23 of this guide.

❶ What is the difference between the mainland Portuguese and those from the island?
a) There is no difference – they have equal rights in all aspects
b) The dialect: people on Madeira speak "high Portuguese"
c) The rock mega-stars don't visit Madeira and there is no IKEA either

❷ What are the main festivals on Madeira?
a) Catholic saints and the island's typical fruits and vegetables are celebrated
b) Cristiano Ronaldo's birthday
c) Every tourism award is honoured with a big celebration

❸ Why is Madeira called the "Island of Flowers"?
a) All year round you will find carpets of flowers as far as the eye can see
b) The island has 800 endemic and over 500 imported plant species
c) Flowers only bloom in May at the annual Flower Festival

❹ Why has emigration always been such a big issue on the island?
a) Because of plagues and pests, natural disasters and economic crises throughout the island's history
b) Because Madeirans can't stand Cristiano Ronaldo any longer
c) Because the weather is better elsewhere

Flower decoration at the annual Flower Festival

❺ Which of these animals are common on Madeira?
a) Fighting bulls, Iberian lynx and Portuguese water dogs
b) Rats, mice and cockroaches
c) Lizards, birds and fish

❻ What does "azulejo" mean?
a) Blue tile
b) Small stone
c) Shining tile

❼ Why are there so many English people on Madeira?
a) Madeira is a British island
b) Many come on holiday, and some have wine-growing businesses on the island
c) They have emigrated there as a result of Brexit

❽ Where are most *quintas* situated?
a) On idyllic rivers
b) On sunny beaches
c) On wet mountain slopes

❾ What does Manueline mean?
a) A decorative technique of the late Gothic period
b) A carving technique of the early Renaissance
c) A Romanesque painting technique

❿ What was the purpose of the first *levadas* in the 15th century?
a) For irrigating the sugar-cane plantations
b) For washing the laundry
c) For trout farming

⓫ What is the secret of Madeira wine?
a) Passion and talent
b) Sugar and cinnamon
c) Heat and time

INDEX

WE WANT TO H EAR FROM YOU!

Did you have a great holiday? Is there something on your mind? Whatever it is, let us know! Whether you want to praise the guide, alert us to errors or give us a personal tip - MARCO POLO would be pleased to hear from you. Please contact us by email:
sales@heartwoodpublishing.co.uk

We do everything we can to provide the very latest information for your trip. Nevertheless, despite all of our authors' thorough research, errors can creep in. MARCO POLO does not accept any liability for this.

PICTURE CREDITS
Cover photo: Funchal, Rua Santa Maria (AWL: F. Vaninetti)
Photos: G. Amberg (131); AWL: P. Adams (12/13, 50), K. Kozlowski (110/111), F. Vaninetti (24/25); DuMont Picture Archive: Leue (8, 76), H. Leue (back cover flap, 102/103); Getty Images/hemis.fr: F. Guiziou (117); R. Hackenberg (86); huber-images: Gräfenhain (6/7, 14/15), G. Gräfenhain (38/39, 138/139); Laif/Hemis: J. Frumm (66); Laif/robertharding: H.-P. Merten (19); S. Lier (143); Look: H. Leue (85); mauritius images (11), Coll (83), S. Hefele (78/79); mauritius images/Alamy (43, 69), W. Jarek (140/141), M. Prusaczyk (31), E. Sergeev (108/109); mauritius images/Alamy/Celos (98/99); mauritius images/Alamy/Hackenberg-Photo-Cologne (outer and inner cover flaps, 1); mauritius images/Alamy/Karol Kozlowski Premium RF (107); mauritius images/Alamy/Mikel Bilbao Gorostiaga-Travels (58/59); mauritius images/Alamy/Panther Media GmbH (88/89, 119); mauritius images/Alamy/Travelpix (20); mauritius images/Alamy/Zoonar GmbH (44, 49); mauritius images/imagebroker: K. Kreder (123); mauritius images/Westend61: J. Stock (10); Schapowalow: L. Debelkova/ (2/3), G. Gräfenhain (53), L. Grandadam (28), S. Wasek (72/73); T. Stankiewicz (9, 27, 30/31, 35, 113); vario images/Imagebroker (23, 47); vario images/Westend61 (32/33); H. Wagner (114/115, 128/129); T. P. Widmann (100); E. Wrba (26/27, 54, 63, 65, 70, 80, 92, 95, 96, 126); Shutterstock/encierro (34)

4th Edition – fully revised and updated 2023
Worldwide Distribution: Heartwood Publishing Ltd, Bath, United Kingdom
www.heartwoodpublishing.co.uk

Authors: Rita Henss, Sara Lier
Editor: Nadia Al Kureischi
Picture editor: Ina-Marie Inderka
Cartography: © MAIRDUMONT, Ostfildern (pp. 36–37, 113, 116, 120, 127, inner flap, outer flap, pull-out map); ©MAIRDUMONT, Ostfildern, using data from OpenStreetMap, Licence CC-BY-SA 2.0 (pp. 40–41, 42, 57, 60–61, 74–75, 90–91, 104–105).
Cover design and pull-out map cover design: bilekjaeger_Kreativagentur with Zukunftswerkstatt, Stuttgart
Page design: Lucia Rojas

Heartwood Publishing credits:
Translated from the German by Thomas Moser, John Sykes, Jennifer Walcoff Neuheiser and Lindsay Chalmers-Gerbracht
Editors: Felicity Laughton, Kate Michell, Sophie Blacksell Jones
Prepress: Summerlane Books, Bath
Printed in India

MARCO POLO AUTHOR
SARA LIER

Along the *levadas*, across the mountains and through the island's parks: whatever the weather, tour guide Sara loves to take her groups on explorative trips around the island. She is passionate about Madeira's lush laurel forests, rugged peaks and magnificent flowers. And she loves the sea, of course, bathing in lava pools whenever possible. Her favourite drink for warming up afterwards is, of course, *poncha*!

DOS & DON'TS

DO DRESS APPROPRIATELY

As with other Portuguese and southern European countries, it's important to be correctly dressed on Madeira. Except on the beach, men should not walk around bare-chested, and many islanders will react with displeasure when women are scantily dressed. Topless bathing is only acceptable around a hotel pool.

DON'T WEAR HIGH HEELS

Madeira is not the place for high heels. Even in the capital, steep slopes and cobble-stones make strolling around a little less smooth than in other cities. Trainers and hiking boots are more suitable than fashionable but impractical footwear.

DO SPEAK PORTUGUESE

Most Portuguese understand Spanish well and know that *Gracias* is easy to say for many tourists. But they will appreciate it when visitors make the effort to say "thank you" in their own language: *Obrigado* (if the speaker is a man) or *Obrigada* (if a woman is speaking).

DON'T UNDERESTIMATE DISTANCES

Measured in kilometres, the distances from A to B on Madeira seem modest. However, almost any journey will encounter ravines and mountains. The number of tunnels is increasing all the time, but in many places the journey still takes you over narrow, steep and winding roads.

DO BE PREPARED FOR FLIGHT DELAYS

It is possible to become stranded on Madeira because all flights have been cancelled. The complex crosswinds sometimes prevent planes from landing at the airport. If this happens, your holiday will be extended by one day – paid for by the relevant airline.